Published in October 2019 by **Dorset Visual Arts**
in association with **Evolver Media**

Foreword by **Professor Anita Taylor**

Design by **Simon Barber**

Edited by **Suzy Rushbrook**

ISBN 978-1-5272-4967-7

Drawing on Dorset

DORSET **VISUAL ARTS** + **EVOLVER**

ARTS UNIVERSITY BOURNEMOUTH

FINE FAMILY FOUNDATION

Supported by **Arts University Bournemouth** and the **Fine Family Foundation**

Printed by **Stephens & George**

DVA Charity Number: 1113249

In Dorset, of Dorset, about Dorset

Foreword

A book of drawings made in relation to a specific place and collected together through an open call - *Drawing on Dorset* - is a unique publication, and a distinctive proposition. The selected drawings made 'in', 'of', and 'about', Dorset all celebrate a breadth of drawing practice, made in response to the creative stimulus of Dorset itself. Here, drawing and the county of Dorset, are simultaneously explored through material investigation and interpretation.

Drawing is a central and pivotal activity to the work of many artists, architects, designers and makers, as a touchstone and tool of creative exploration that informs visual discovery, enabling the visualisation and development of perceptions and ideas. Used both as a means to encounter and examine the world, and as a departure point for new understanding and identification of subject and content to be explored, drawing remains a fundamental means to translate, document, record and analyse our experiences of the worlds we inhabit. With a history as extensive as the history of our cultures, the act of drawing enables new insights and understanding of our current perceptions of place and experience, and in a range of ways.

The drawings included here represent a panoply of approaches, of direct and indirect reference and inspiration, and include observational, documentary, experiential and imaginative responses inspired by being in, or reflecting on, a county renowned for its natural beauty. It is evidently a place that inspires artists and makers to live and sustain their practice there, referential or not, as much as it is a site that inspires exploration and depiction of this exquisite landscape or coastline, or an event or experience of travel itself; it also provides a locus for the investigation of, and response to, current or historical ideas and issues, be they environmental, political or personal. Each of these individual perspectives enable us to see drawing, and Dorset, anew.

Professor Anita Taylor
Director, Drawing Projects UK

Make a mark

Make a mark

Leave trace

Something against nothing

Drawing for me provides a focus, something to rest on, a place to drop anchor. Every drawing inadvertently becomes a diary of the time spent making it. For the last decade I have made my home in the southwest, an abundant, soft and welcoming place with a connection to deep timelines still living and running through it.

Not living in a city has meant I understand how deep the divisions are on this small island between rural and urban, and how unwise it is to generalize about the non-urban, where profoundly conservative and continuous approaches to life sit alongside the radical rural - and everything has to make peace with the weather.

I am an un-rooted wanderer by nature and the only place that I can really call home is my work. I know there is an exchange with where I am every time I make a drawing. Places flow through you as you move through them.

This collection of drawings charts the expanded field of drawing that relates to place: Dorset, a tidal county that swells with visitors during holiday times and goes quiet in the low tides of winter. The drawings in this book revel a range of complex relationships with a place that map, excavate and chart both the hefted deep connections of memory and experience, alongside the flux of place, as unstable as the cliffs.

A sense of place is a route to access a sense of self. So many of these drawings are searching, whether charting sound, beach-combing, intensely observing the skin of a cliff or tree, a memory of childhood or mothering, psychedelic landscapes of the interior, light across water, or litter at the edge of the field. The range of subjects is mirrored in the diversity of ways of making a drawing, inking meat to print from, filmed performative marks, stitched contours, burning lines with the sun, or a simple pencil line.

Drawing develops perspective, distance and intimacy. Making a drawing is an experience of being intensely present. This is compelling collection of drawings that celebrates in so many varied, relevant and subtle ways the place of presence in drawing practice today.

Tania Kovats

Artist and Professor of Drawing at Bath Spa University

Amanda Wallwork

Lost Field 1883: Jeffery's Close

Drawing is fundamental to much of my work - the act of making the mark part of the concept. Whether representing paths, track ways, boundaries or borders the physical process of successive drawing, erasing and repeatedly re-drawing a line replicates the act of walking or marking out the earth.

Graphite, oil and plaster on board, 40 x 50 x 4 cm

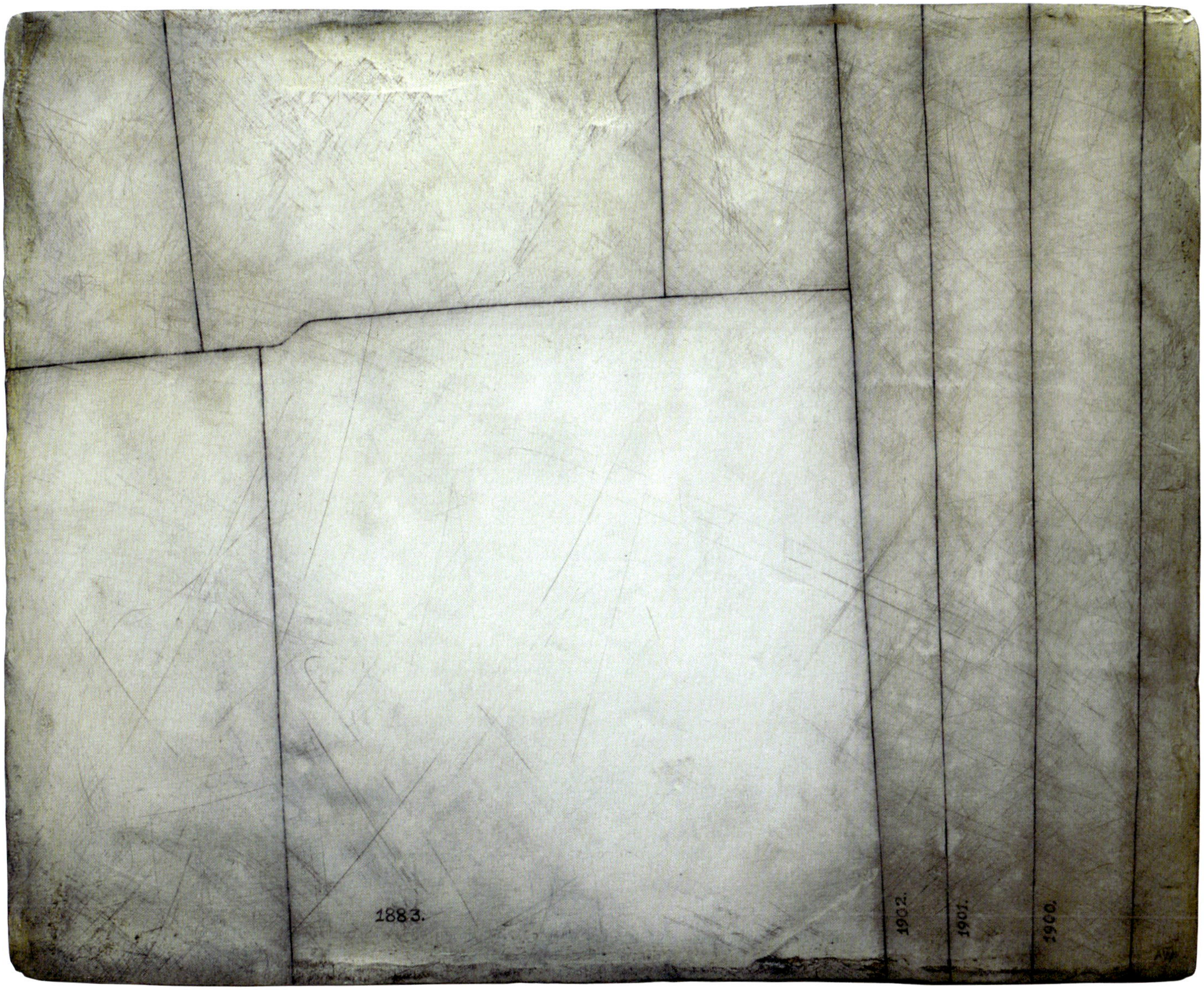
1883.
1902.
1901.
1900.

Andy Fung

Yin Yang Waves

My drawings and paintings grow out of initial mark making into complex psychedelic and futuristic works. The work has an infinitesimal quality and refers to pop art, graffiti, sci-fi illustration and '60s psychedelia. This drawing relates to trips to coastal National Trust land near Weymouth and the rhythm of the waves.

Pencil on canvas, 20 x 40 cm, 2018

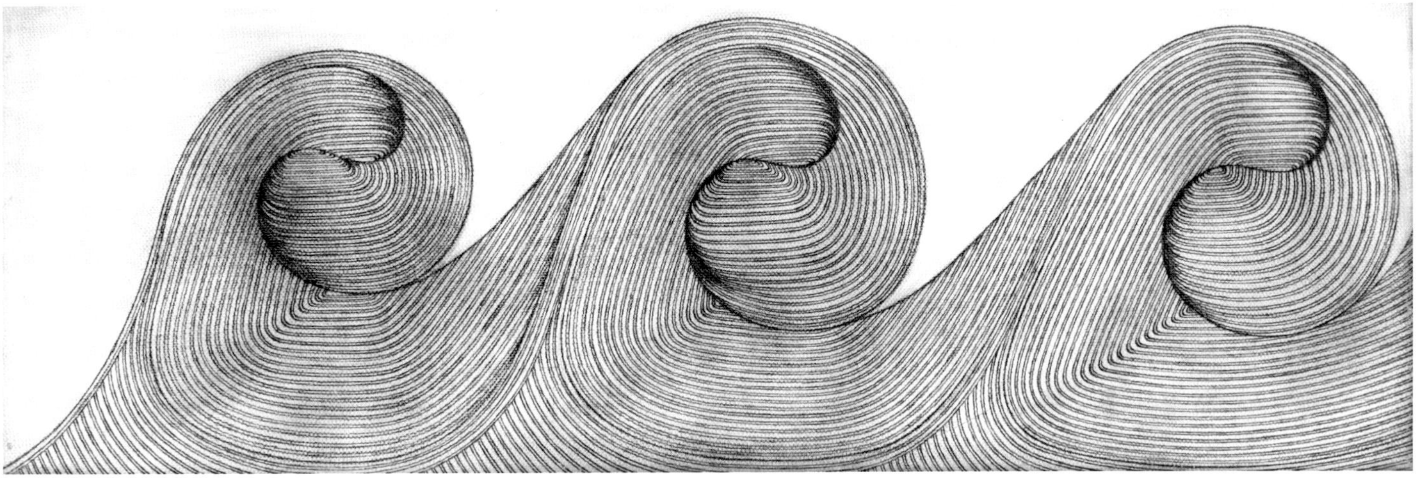

Angela Charles

Risking it at West Bay

I created this work after a walk along Chesil Beach at West Bay, where warnings of unstable cliffs dare you to walk on the beach beneath them.

Acrylic and coloured pencil on aluminium panel, 51 x 51 cm, 2016

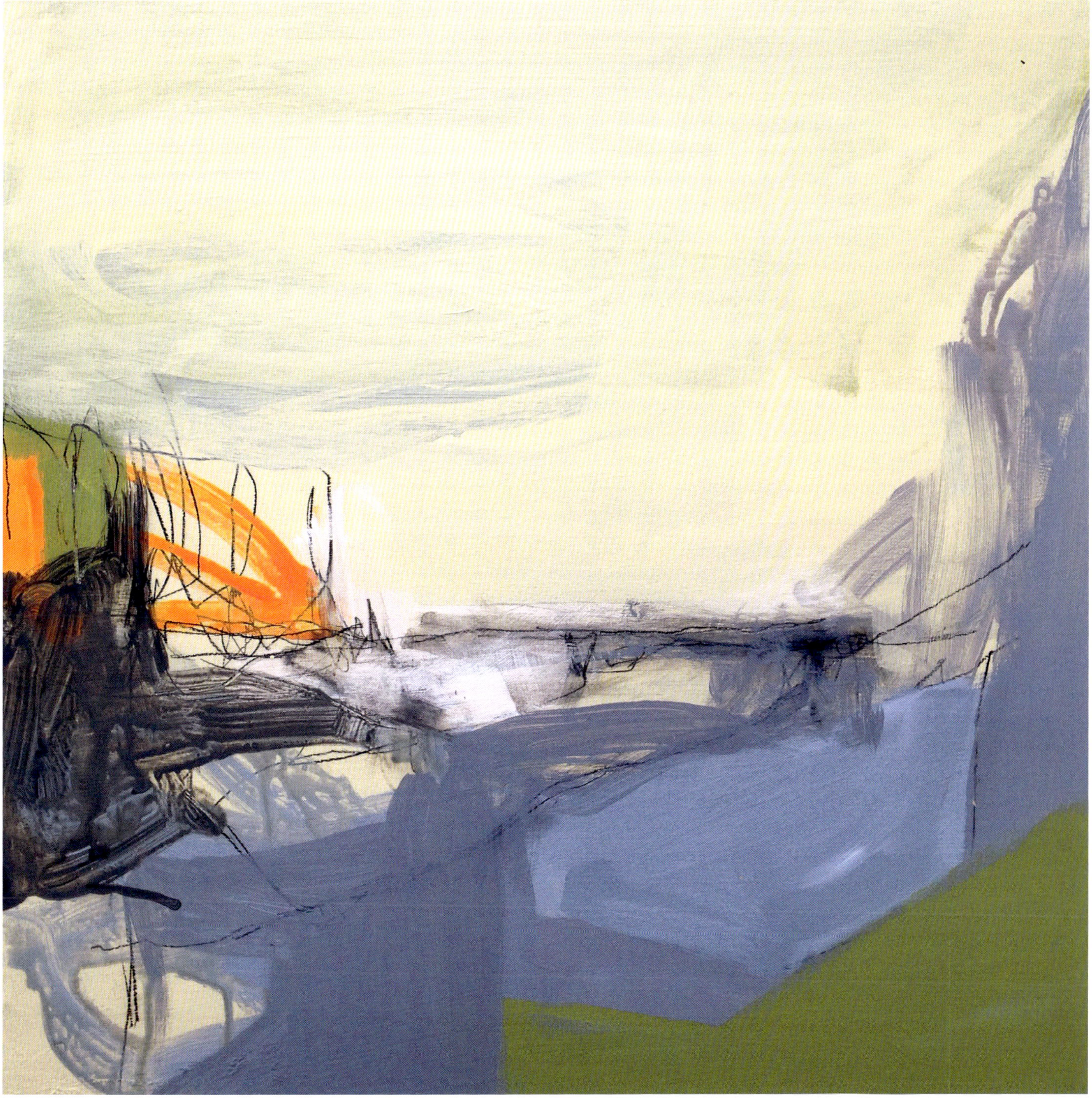

Anna Morris

Landforms 3

My work explores the transformative effect of light, investigating mark-making and referencing landscape through drawing, painting and collage. I aim to create still and contemplative works that evoke the experience of visual phenomena – of atmospheric light and luminosity – whilst drawing attention to the processes involved in their making.
I draw with collaged papers, oil soaked and marked with a range of processes using a knife and occasionally thread to articulate the surface of my work.

Oil, ink, household paint on paper, 18 x 16 cm, 2019

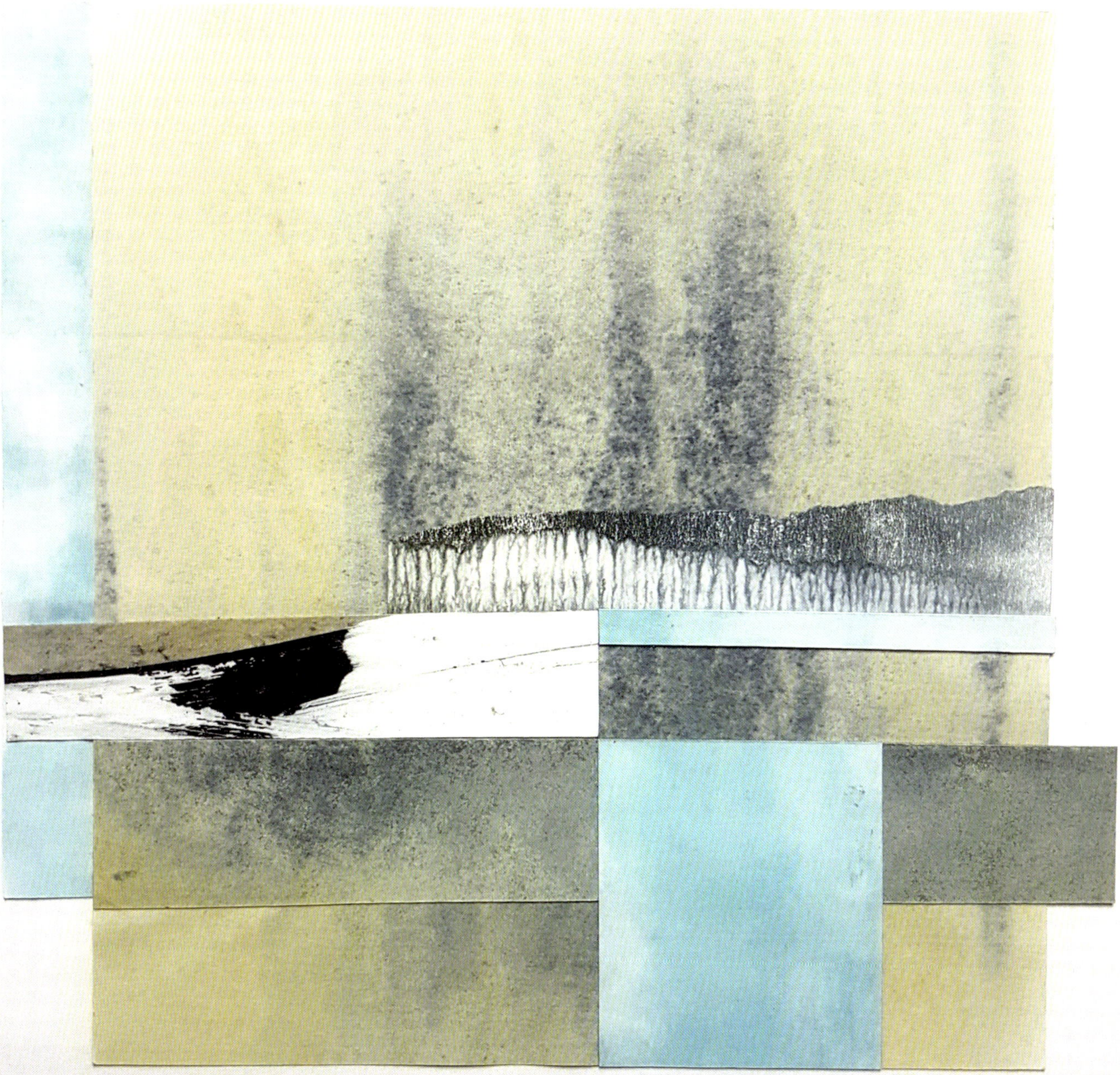

Bonnie Brown

Tonal Pulse

Living and working in Purbeck, interested in the fragility of light and water, their effects and qualities of transience and transformation. Observations of the shoreline, the liminal boundary between land, sea and air, the static and the moving. Contrasts, dualities, tonal values and the emotional connection found in this landscape.

Charcoal and mixed media on paper, 75.5 x 75.5 cm, 2018

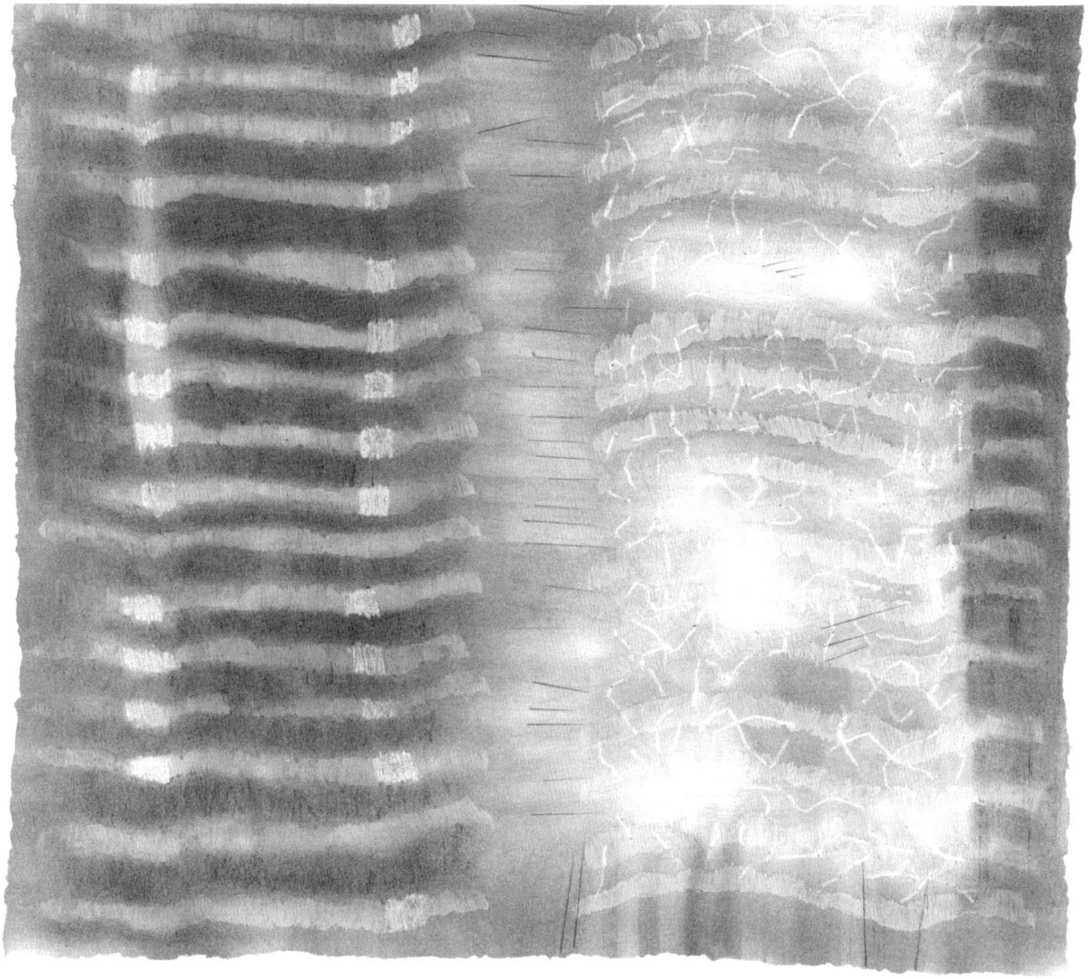

Caroline Liddington

Memory Interior 1

I am influenced by the spaces I inhabit and the 'framed' views beyond, keenly interested in depth, contrast and unexpected vistas, as seen through doorways and windows. My recent work explores the pictorial quality of memory. This drawing begins a new series, stimulated by childhood impressions of domestic spaces.

4B + 6B pencil on paper, 57 x 76 cm, March 2019

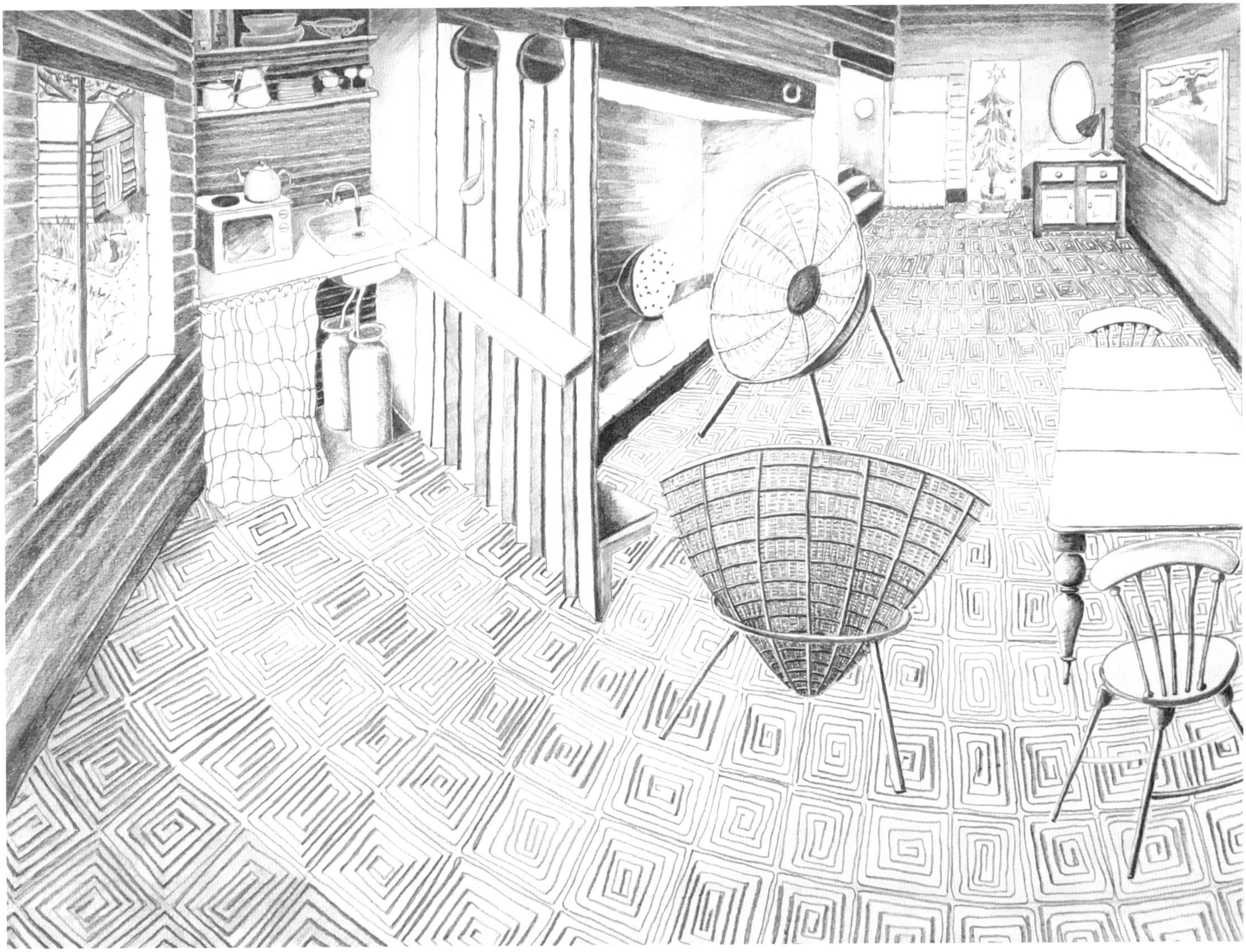

Carrie Mason

Marking Time, 2018

pause

breathe

notice

mark

repeat

reflect

Exploring the challenges of living in contemporary society by reconnecting with the physicality of materials and our senses. A sense of place, a sense of time and a sense of self.

Still from durational drawing performance documentation video
7 minutes 30 seconds

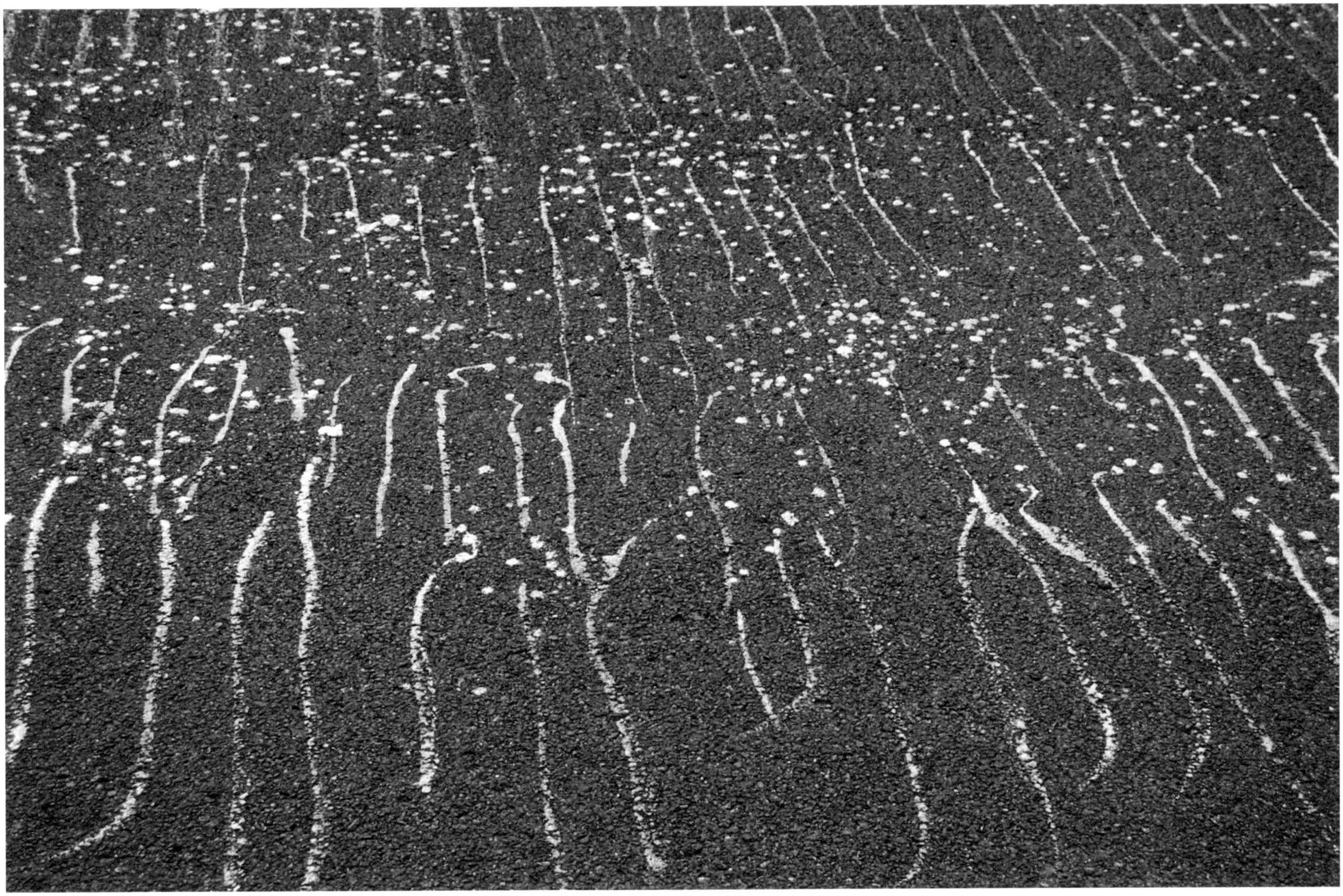

Chris Dunseath
Dorset Periphery

Dorset Periphery develops a two-dimensional diagrammatic representation of the county border into an imaginary three-dimensional form. A slow, intensive and intricate use of graphite, carefully applied and also erased, gradually evolved into an image resembling a receptacle structure, suggesting a repository of both complex geological time and cultural layering.

Graphite on 300gsm Arches paper, 45 x 30 cm, 2019

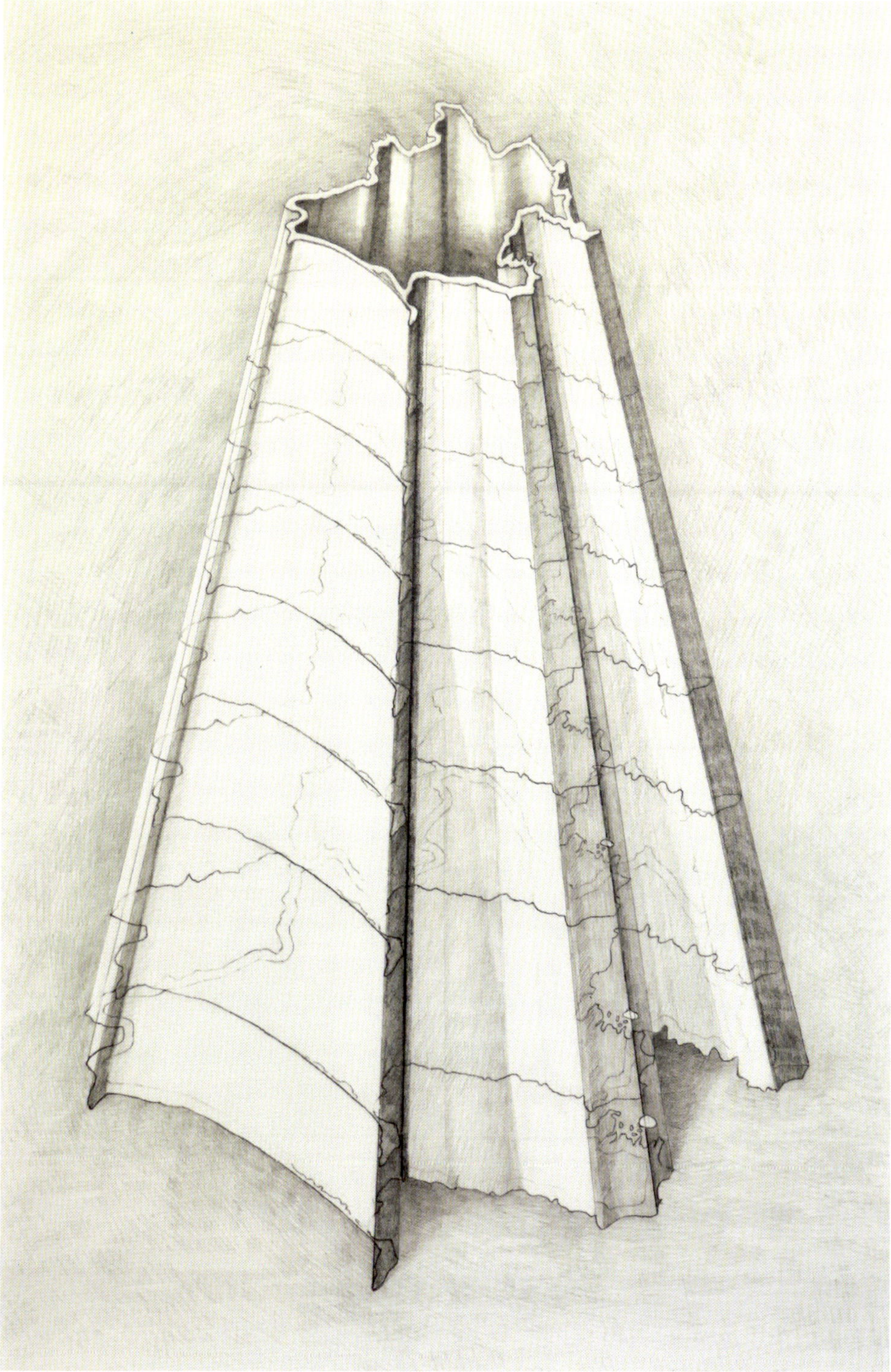

David Atkins

Lake on Middlebere Heath Dorset III

The immediacy of drawing allows me to think quickly and respond with a directness that engages me completely. There is a freedom to explore, play, take chances, meet challenges and lose everything without fear. My drawings are made from a subject and give clues to my thinking and feelings about it.

Ink, acrylic, watercolour, charcoal, 100 x 135 cm, July 2018

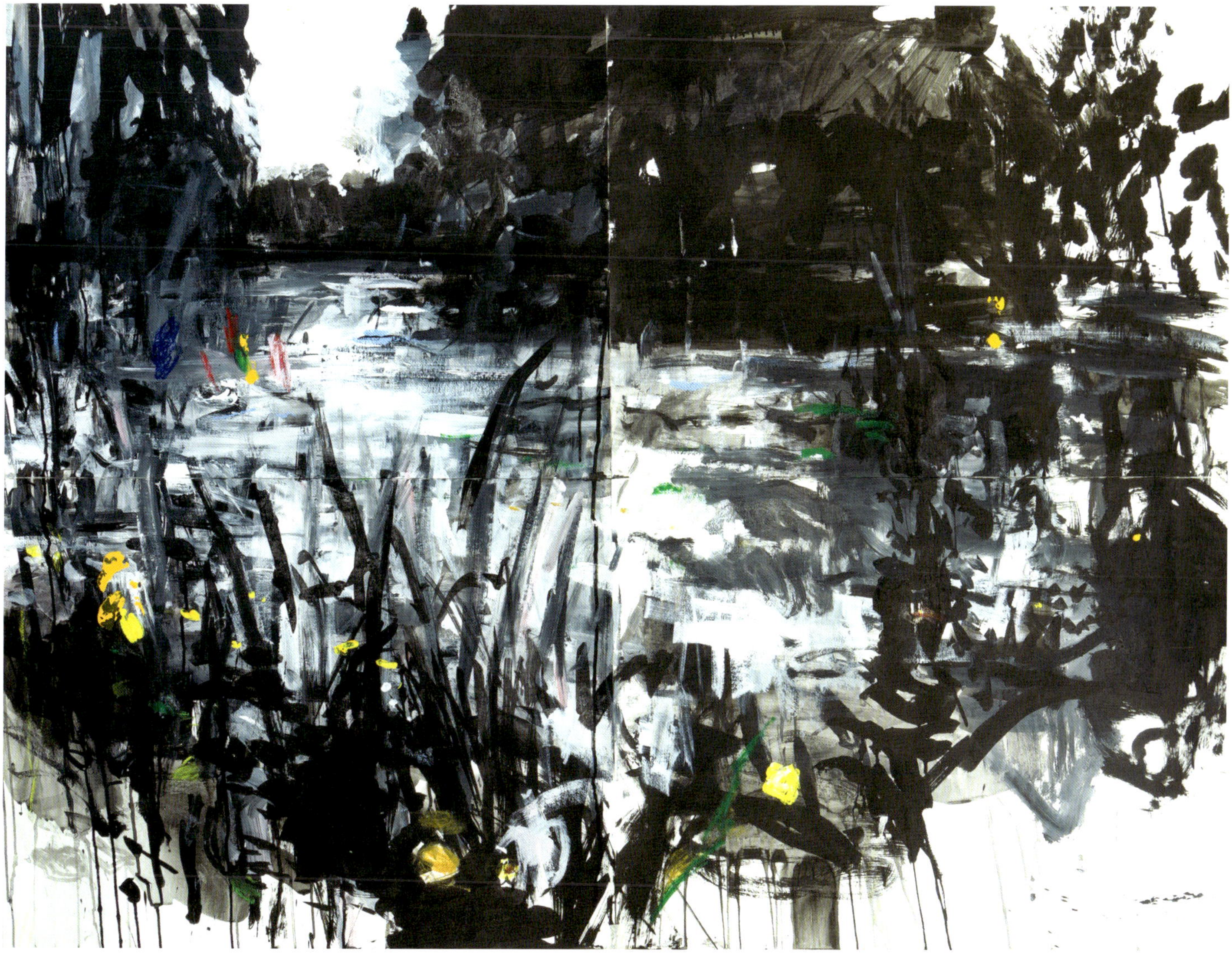

Day Bowman

Study 2 Plashy Place

In these small scale drawings on canvas the marks, lines and shapes echo those that we made into the wet grey sand of our hometown beach in childhood; the calligraphic marks celebrate the simple lugworm, tide pools and strange cliff findings along the coast of Dorset.

Oil, charcoal and conte on canvas, 45 x 50 x 4 cm, 2019

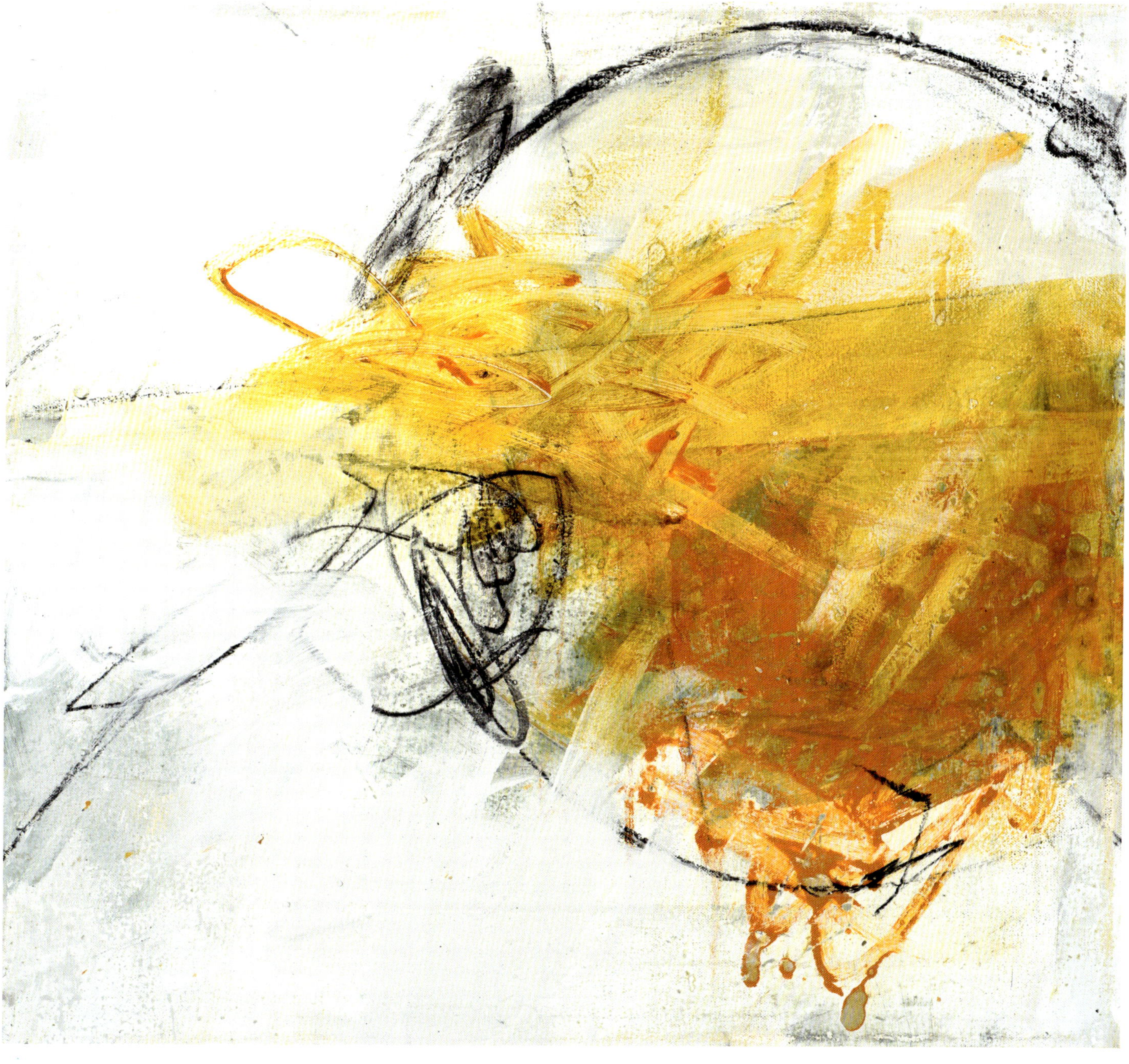

Debbie Lee
Levitation

Levitation is a drawing from an animation made by erasing and redrawing images. It symbolises the balance between art-making and parenting and illustrates a childhood memory of trying to levitate between 2 chairs but always caving in as the chairs pulled further apart. In art the impossible can be achieved.

Charcoal on paper, 60 x 73 cm, April 2018

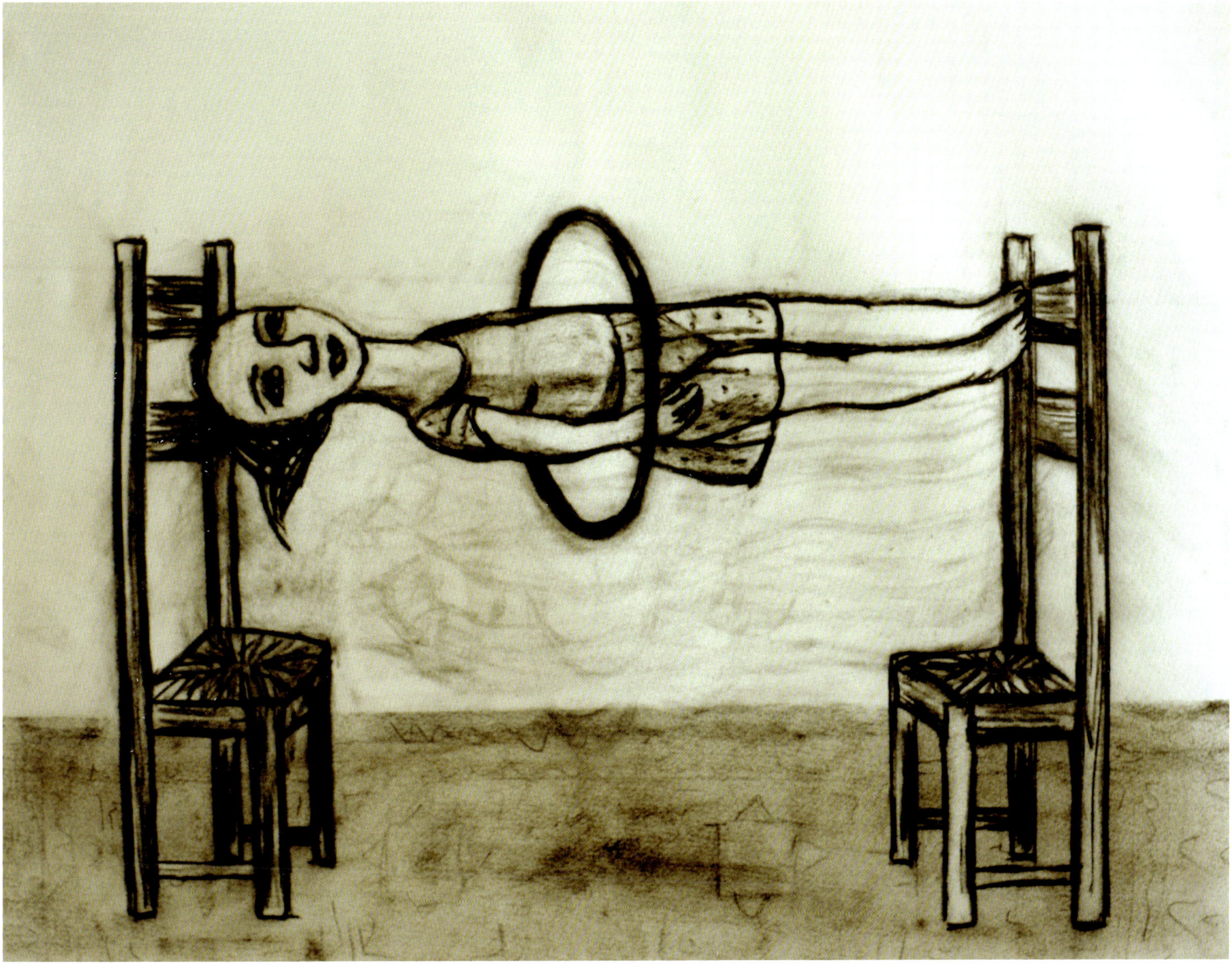

Ed Frith

Working Drawing 19

Working Drawing 19 or *Hyperloop Hardy* is a drawn psycho-geographic mapping, past and future, from the Dorset Cursus and the 'antique brown' of 'Egdon Heath' to a bio-physical future. Key references for the drawing are the work of the biologist and planner, Patrick Geddes, and Felix Guattari's book, *The Three Ecologies*.

Ink, conte, on cartridge, 29.8 x 59.6 cm, March 2019

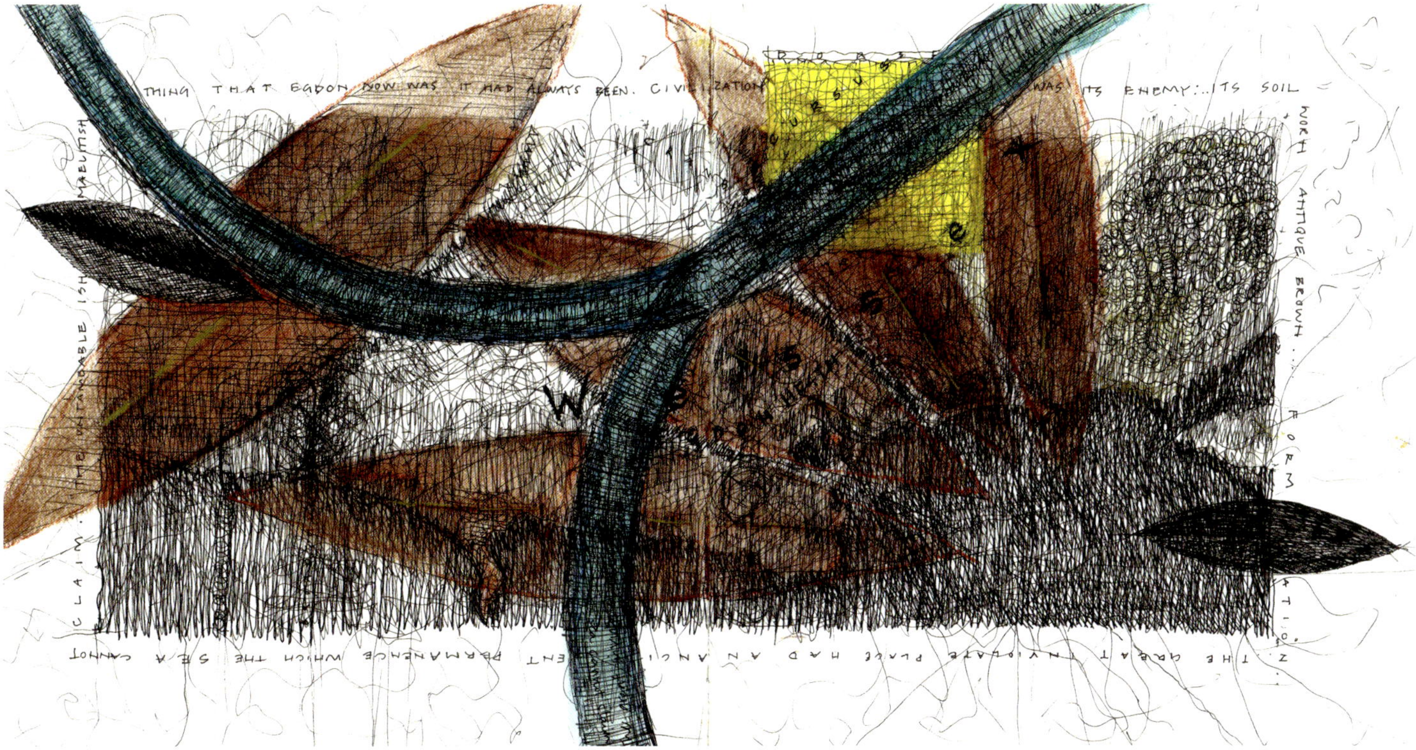
THING THAT EGDON NOW WAS IT HAD ALWAYS BEEN. CIVILIZATION
WAS ITS ENEMY:..ITS SOIL
WORN ANTIQUE BROWN... FORM
THE GREAT INVIOLATE PLACE HAD AN ANCI ENT PERMANENCE WHICH THE SEA CANNOT
CLAIM. THE UNTAMEABLE ISHMAELITISH

Elaine Collett

Crop Lines 2

Clearly visible shreds of plastic, lengths of baler twine and plastic detritus of indeterminate origin, lie alongside flints amongst the winter wheat. Vistas of plenty and beauty hide litter amongst the weed at the edge of the crop.

Mono print composite drawing incorporating text, 46 x 61 cm
February / March 2019

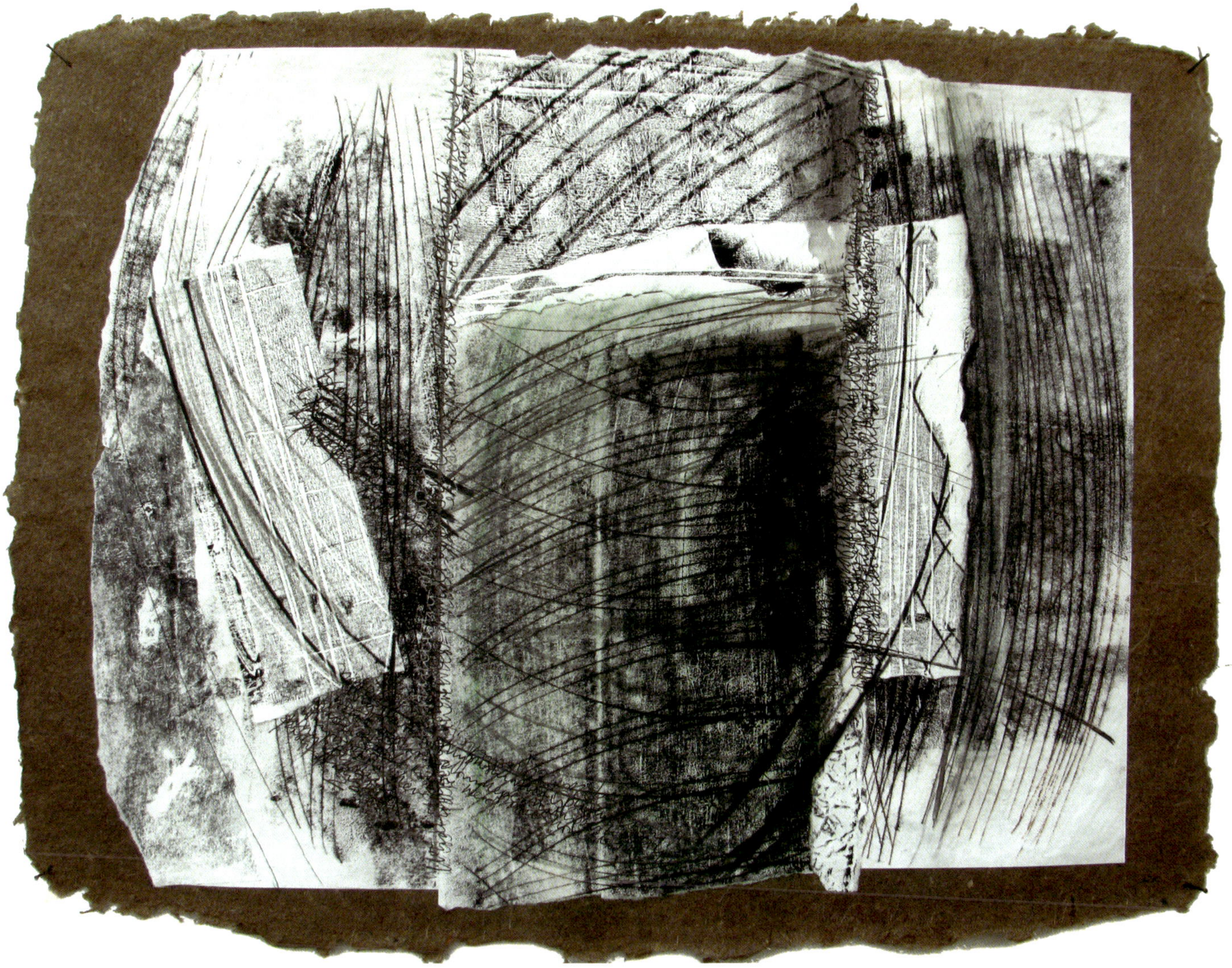

Emma Davies

Sounds of Sidhe

I am a multi-disciplinary artist whose work encompasses performance, live art, installation, mixed media, and drawing. *Sounds of Sidhe* are two site responsive and time based drawings; drawing sound through movement to evoke sense of place, time, and to describe emotional connections to a personal setting within the Purbecks.

Charcoal on Fabriano, 60 cm x 109.5 cm, 'Dusk' 22 February 2019 + 'Midday' 23 February 2019

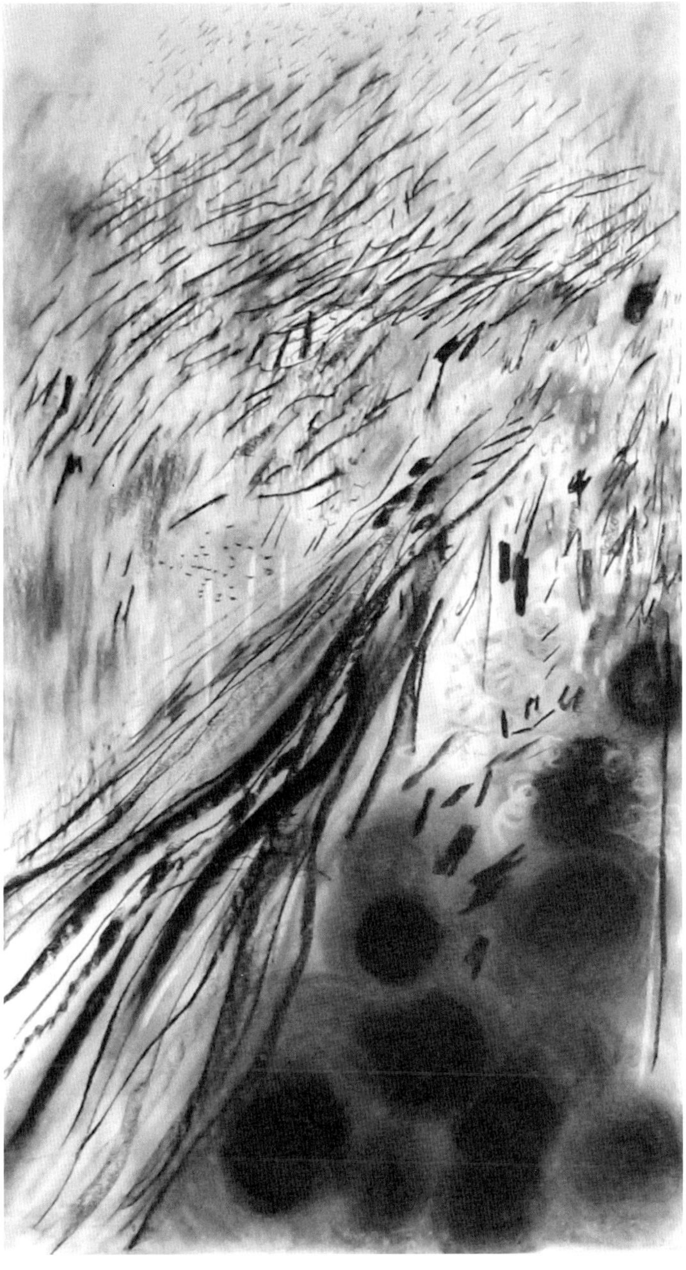

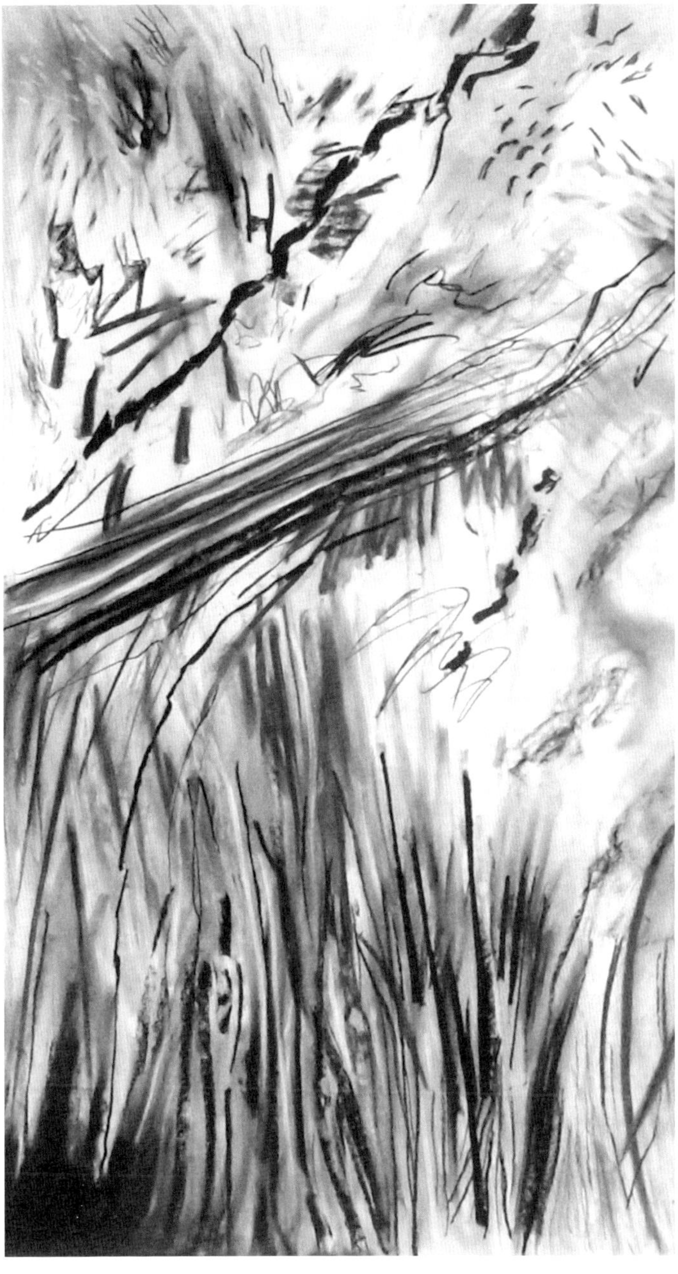

Fay Stevens

Swanage Old Pier

The old pier is a ruin suspended in the liquidity of Swanage Bay. My father, a geologist, and I spend many hours walking, looking and talking about the deep time history of this area of the Dorset landscape. It is an ongoing conversation between geology and archaeology, father and daughter.

Drawing with permatrace, charcoal, pipette and seawater from Swanage Bay, A2

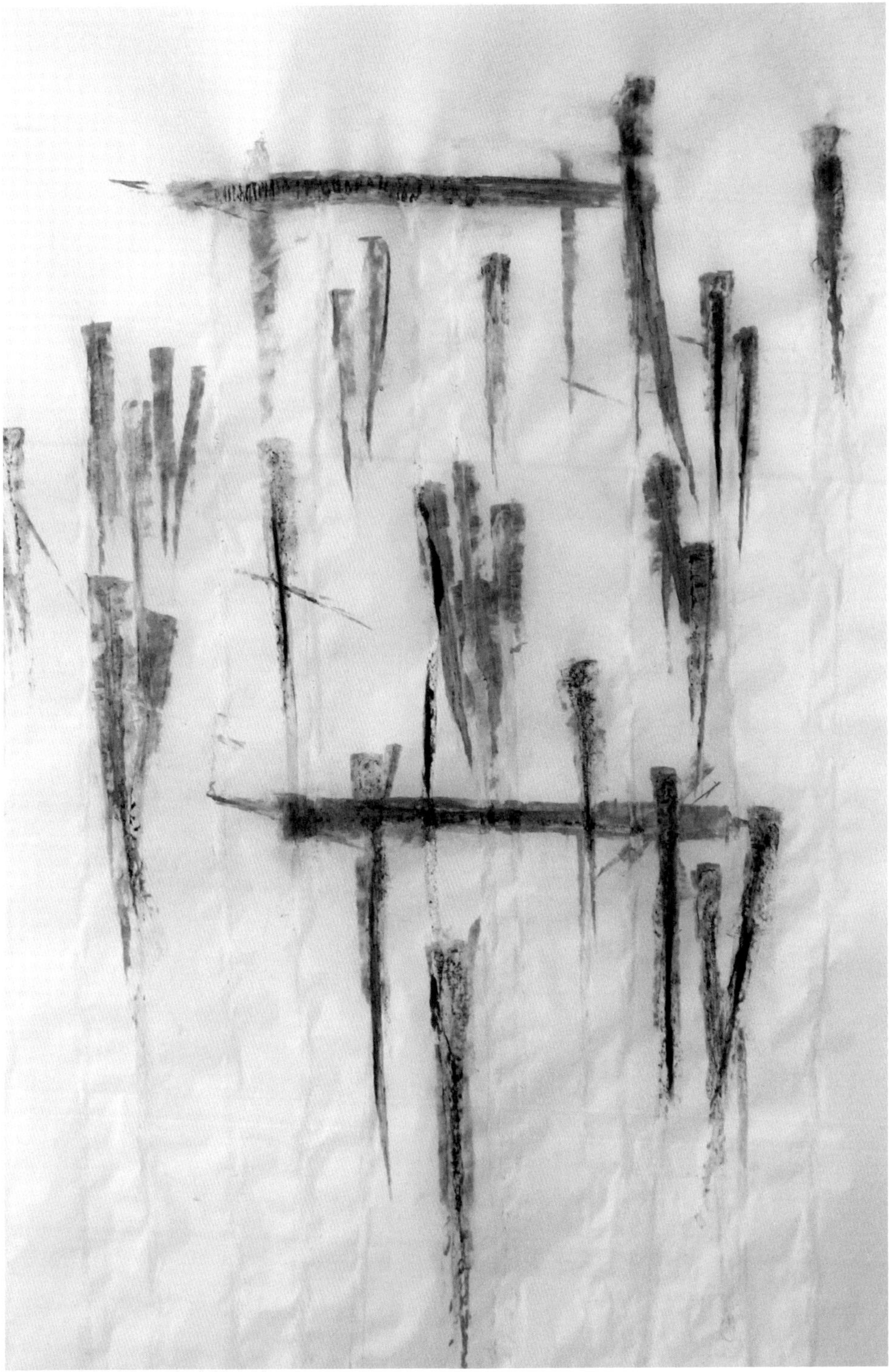

Faye Bowden

Growth II

The *Growth* series (ongoing) began whilst I was in residence at The Royal Drawing School studios at Dumfries House, Scotland in March 2018. After a pause in my creative practice the series has become a metaphor for my state of self, whilst also challenging the concept of space on paper.

Pencil on paper, 84.1 x 59.4 cm, 2018

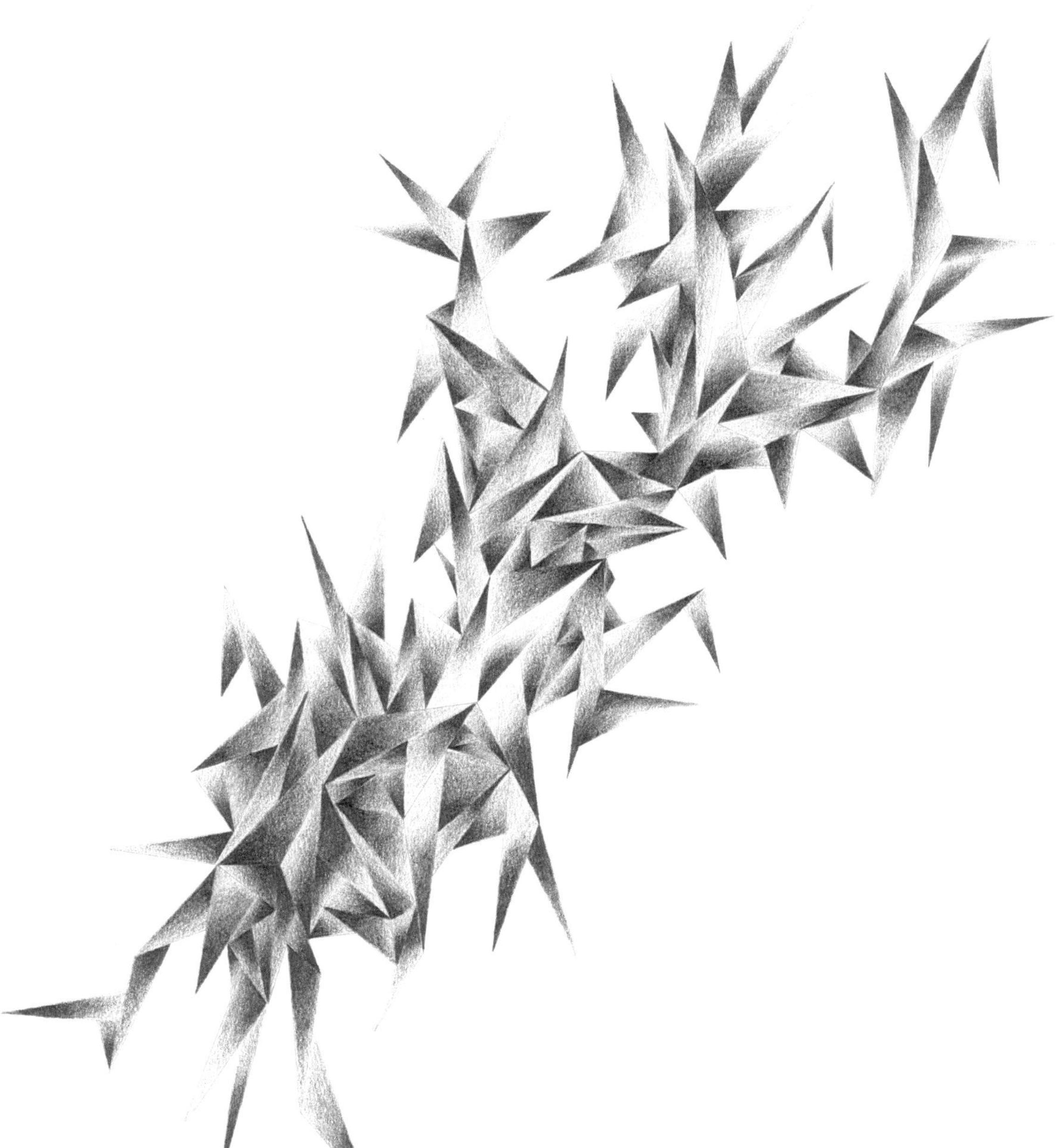

Fiona Campbell

Traces

Treating line as object, my work intersects sculpture, drawing and installation. Interconnections from micro to macro, nature's cyclical persistence and transformation inform my practice, in which materiality and process are central. Often labour-intensive, my use of recycled and found materials relates to waste, our relationship with matter, nature, and ourselves.

Copper wire, handmade khadi paper, linseed oil, rabbit skin glue, sisal, wall paper paste, 140 x 116 x 12 cm, 2017

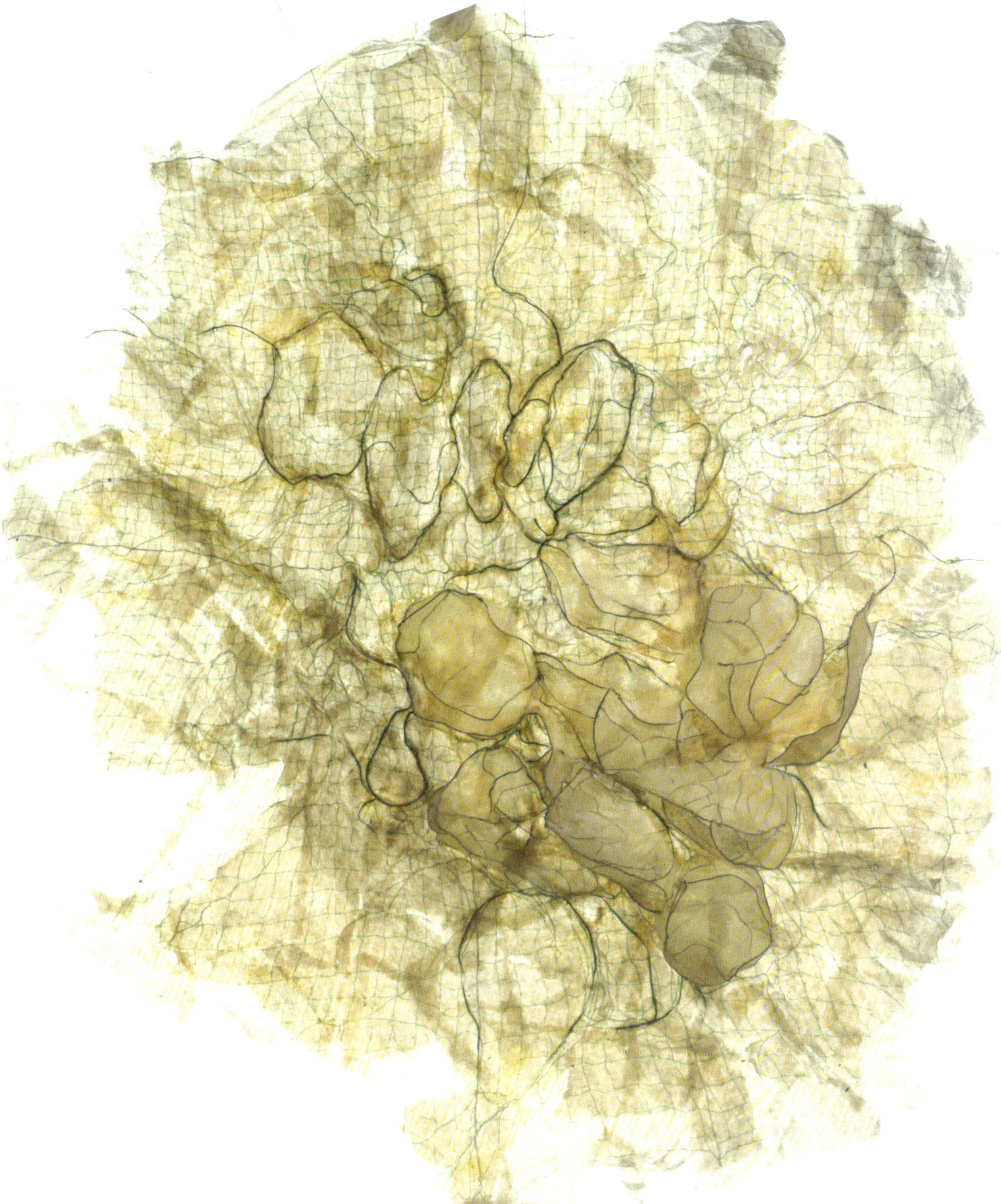

Fiona Robinson

La Mer Debussy

My work is increasingly informed by music. Using the language of drawing I create an equivalent of, a transcription of, music. It is not a system of notation; not an alternative to a musical score to be reinterpreted; it is a response to the sound. My drawings present a communication between composer and artist, a conversation between two practitioners, through the languages they use to express their ideas.

Graphite, charcoal and mixed media, 80 x 120 cm, 2016

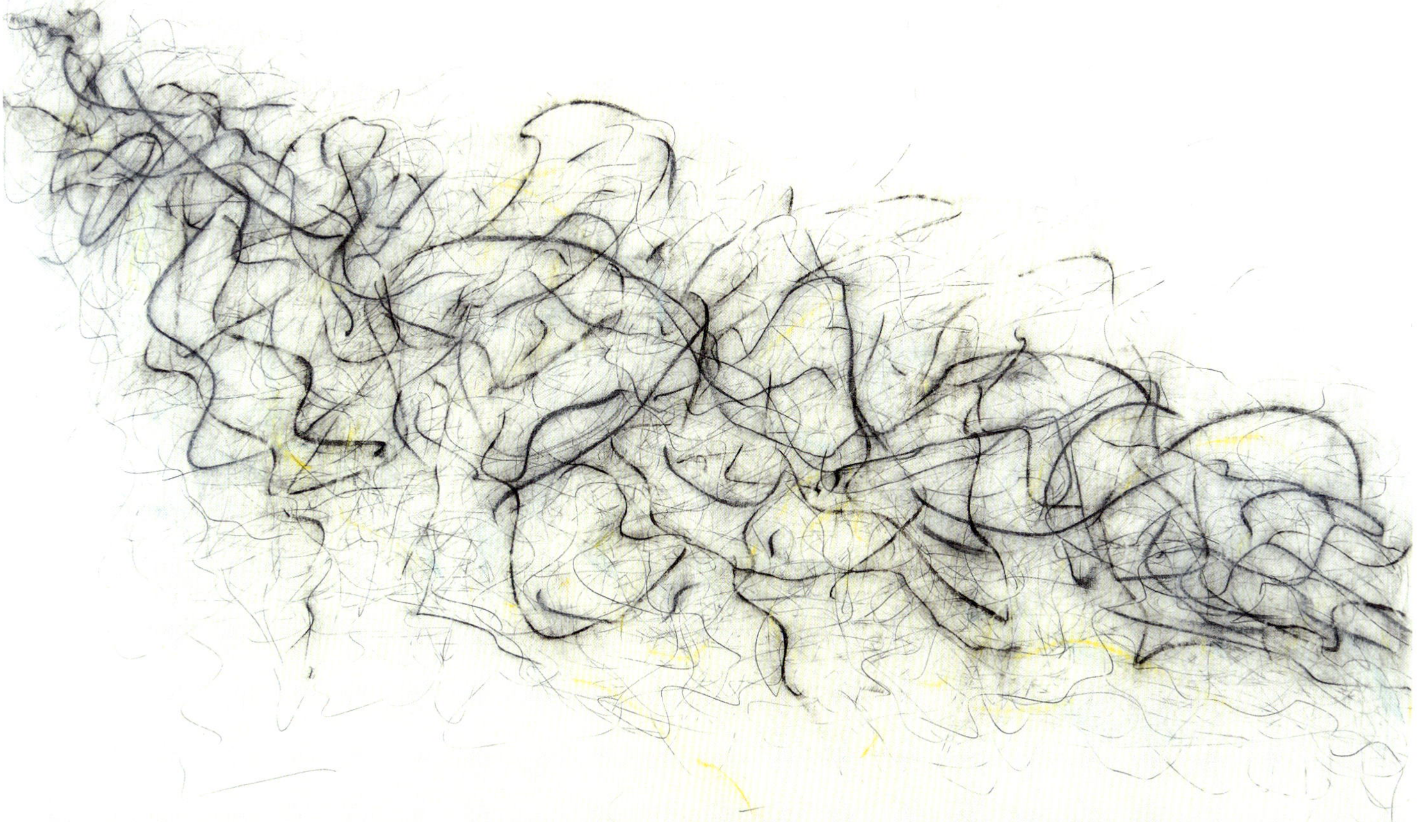

Fran Norton

Dorset 1

This print-based drawing arose from questioning the tenuous ecological and creative relationships between rural Dorset and its inhabitants. As the flesh of locally-reared livestock is repeatedly inked up then hand-pressed on paper, an imagining mind strives to read hills, cliffs, rocks, fields and sand into the 'invertible landscapes' that result.

Relief print (locally sourced meat) and ink, 105 x 148 mm, 2019

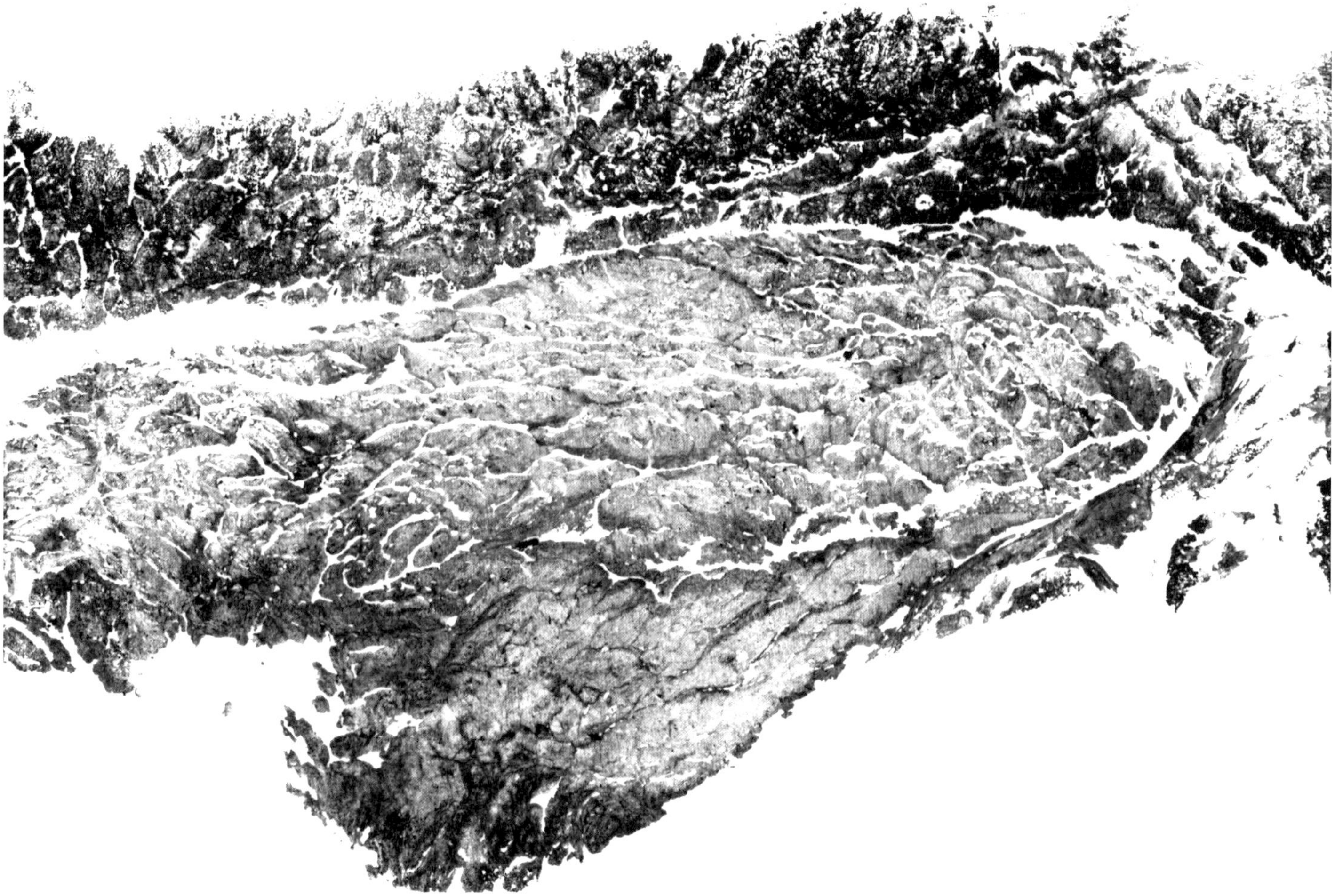

Fran Quinlan

Agitated State

I use the body as a means of exploring the visceral, which reacts and responds to states of being human. Drawing is an integral part of my practise that pulls together my thoughts and emotions. I use charcoal, thread and ink because they resonate with my gut feelings.

Charcoal, 31 x 21 cm, 2019

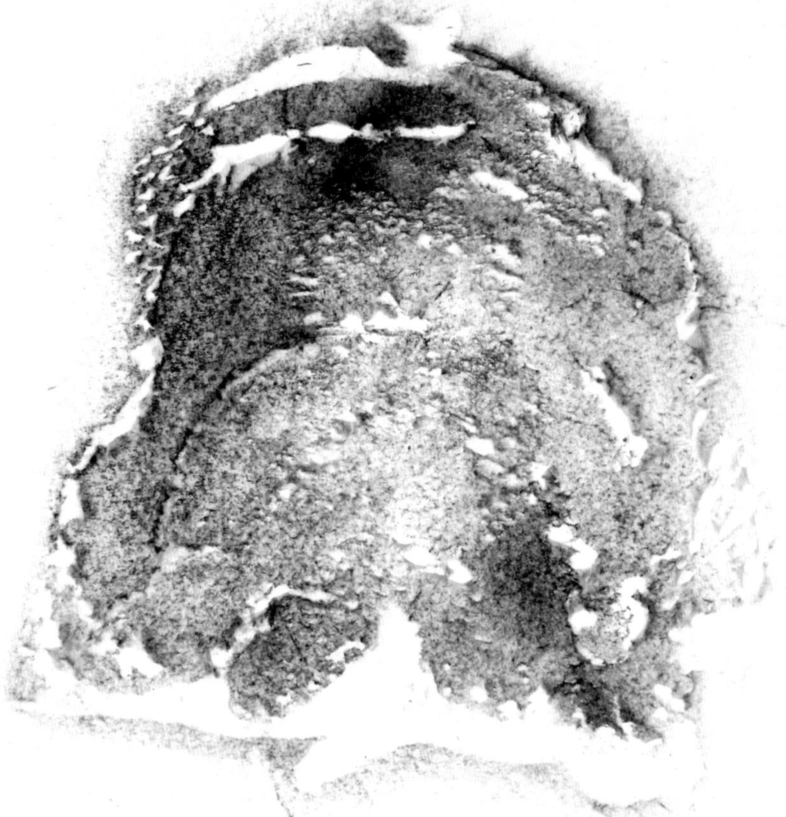

Frances Hatch

The Uncomformity in the Armpit of South Beach, Studland

South Beach provides pigment and tools. Weather, tide and season animate, reveal and conceal. I document, collect, participate, play. Materials shift hourly, yearly and over millennia. Work is generated en plein air: site materials enter and inhabit the work: each piece is particular and provisional. Cellophane sits with the Cenozoic.

Foraged beach materials on handmade indian paper, 36 x 72 cm
29 January 2019

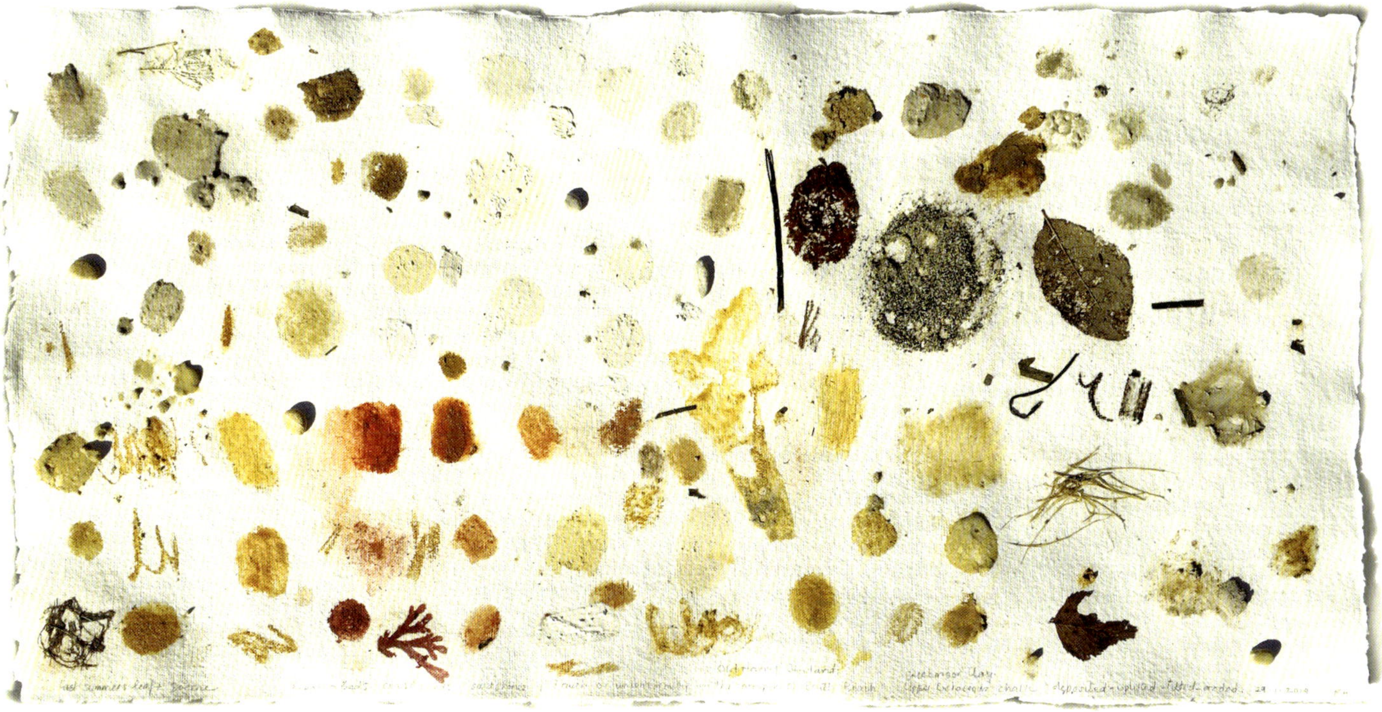

Helen Dean

Durlston Cliff

My work seeks to depict the essential structure and strength of the natural environment, showing the immense power of nature over time. The fault lines, strata and patterns created by erosion, the play of light, tone and texture, and the geological forms of the coastline are what interest me most.

Dip pen and Indian ink, 31 x 43 cm, 2018

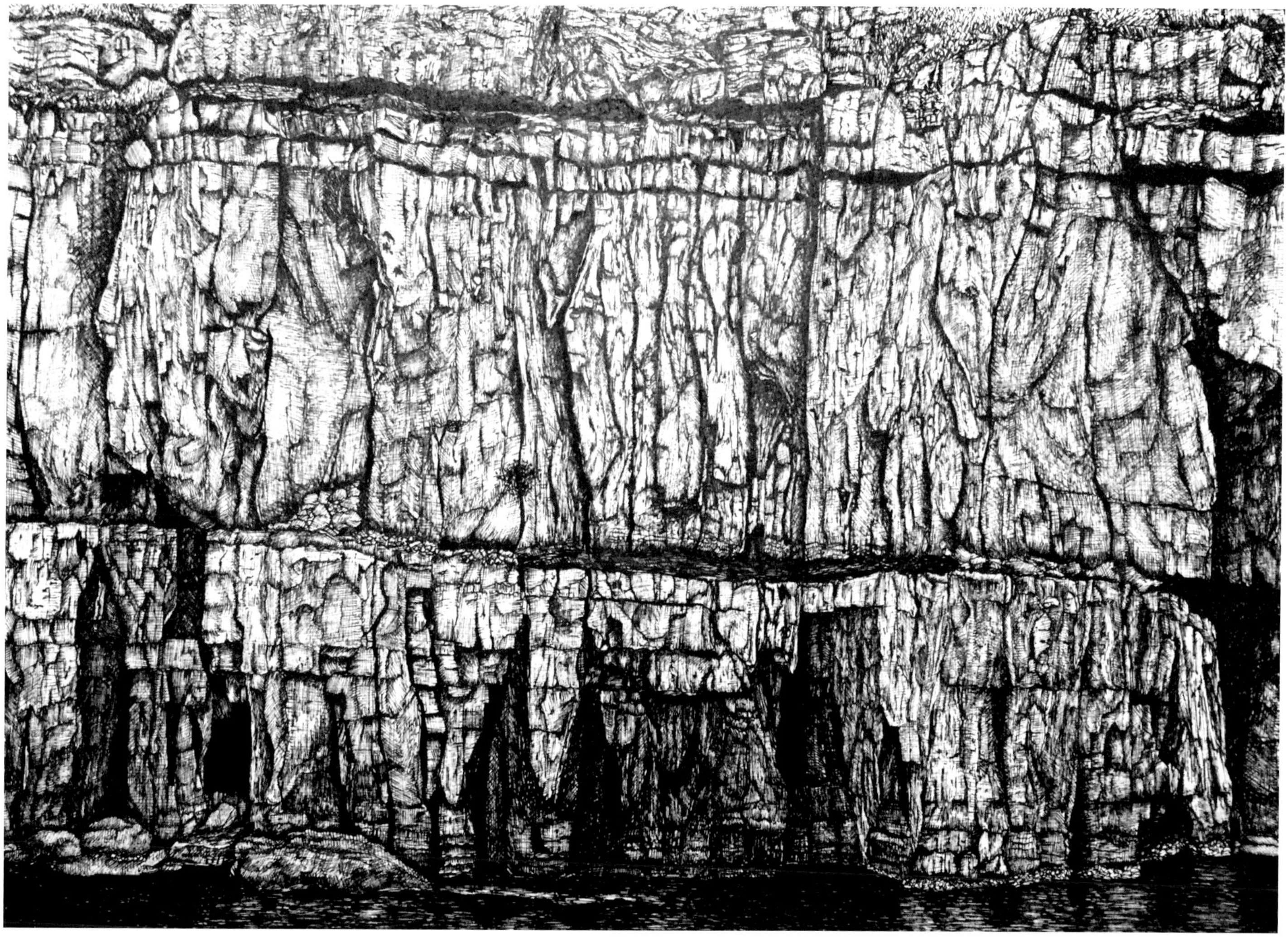

Helen Simpson
Snapdragon

Do we share the same physiology with plants? The taut shapes, creases, veins and tubular structures within the petals of this snapdragon, to me suggest aspects of human anatomy. To the viewer they may evoke different associations.

Graphite on paper, 40 x 28 cm, 2017

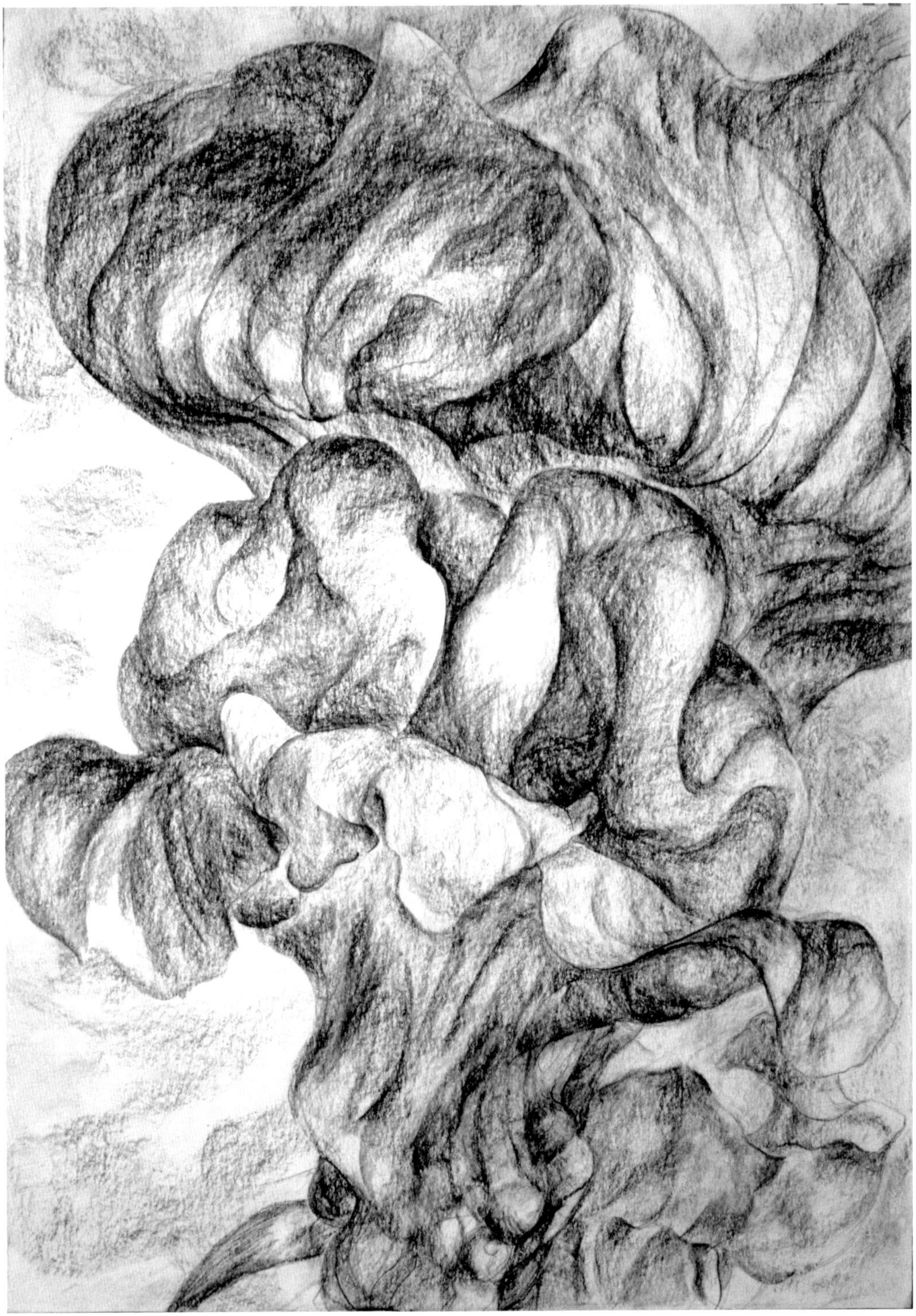

Holly Yates

Chesil Cove

Hand-stitched linear graphics are collaged with painted embroidery on canvas. Diluted acrylic paint is sprayed and dripped, and allowed to flow and settle around textural stitched marks. Many images of Chesil focus on the shoreline, but for me it is the rocky tumbling stone cliffs that dominate the scene.

Cotton and acrylic on canvas and paper, 56 x 76 cm, 2019

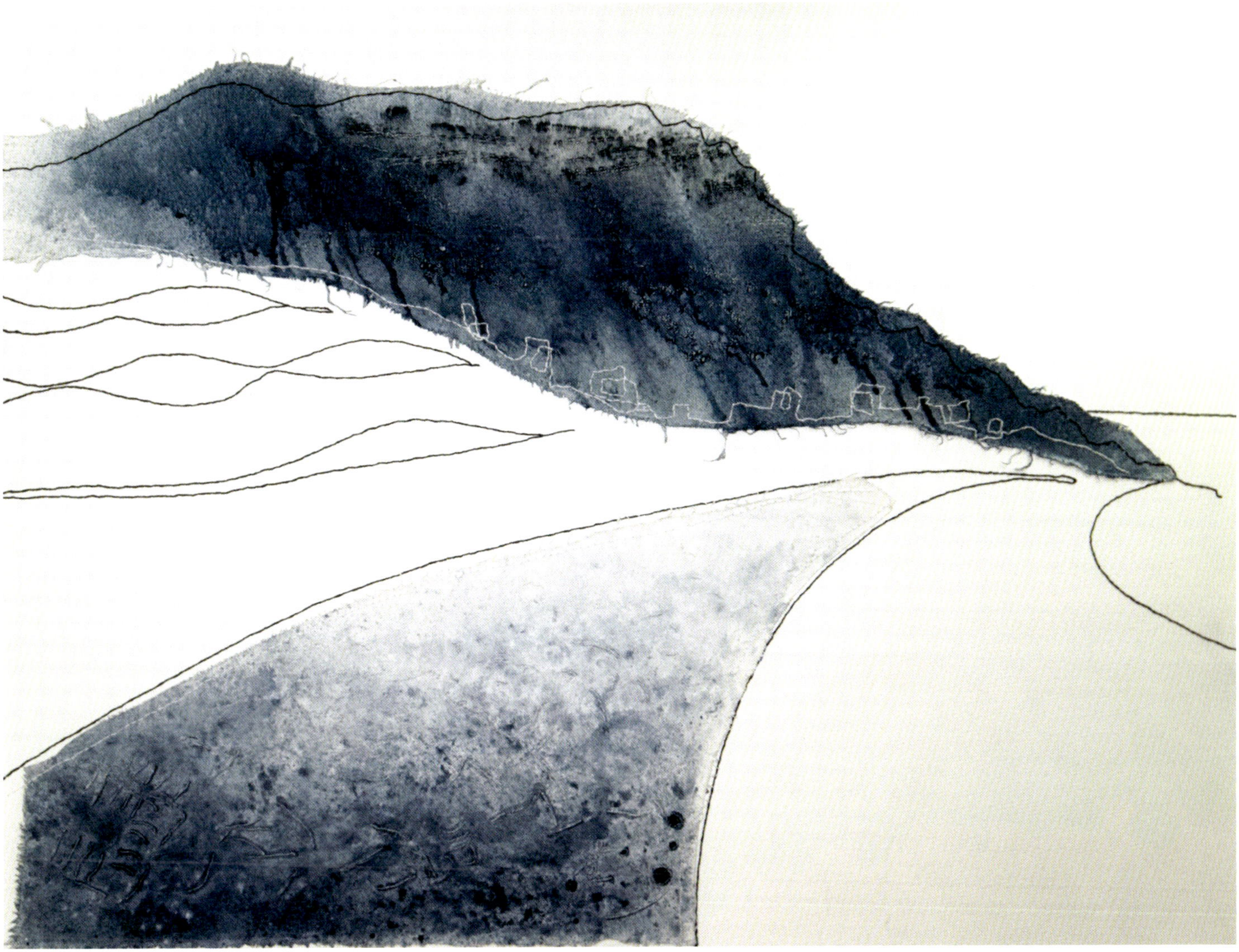

Ilona Skladzien

YouTube II

While my attention is occupied by explicit YouTube videos of the poultry industry my drawings morph into doodles. Bringing a flow to the paper, the unconscious and the illogical connects myself and my doodles to the moving image of the horrific content presented.

Rollerball pen on canvas textured paper, 24 x 37 cm, 2019

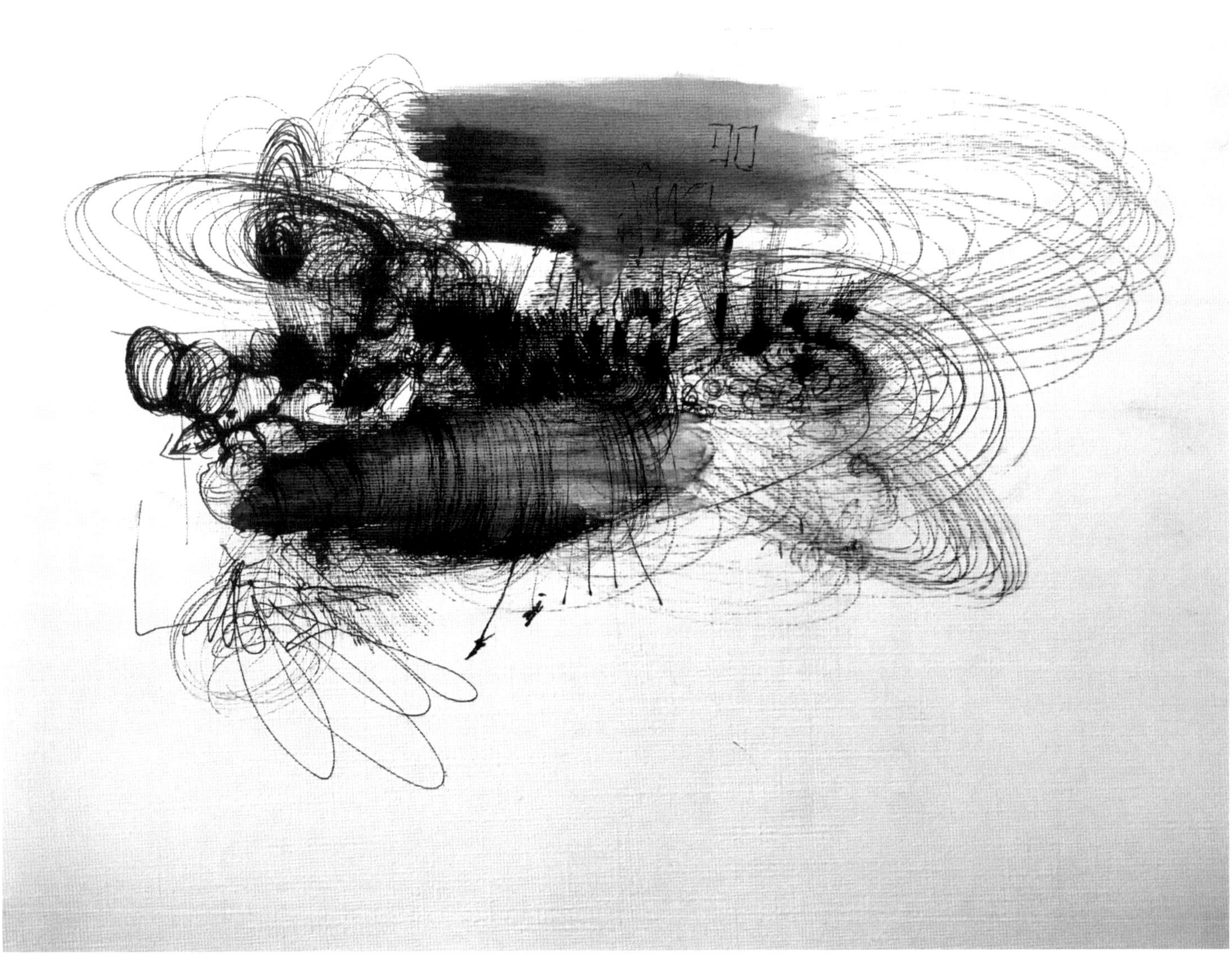

Jem Main

Migration, Myth, Metaphor

The drawing belongs to an on-going series of works sparked by an archeology programme illuminating relationships between the Vikings and Picts. It includes 3D drawings and reliefs. The series - and the motifs - reference deep-felt cultural influences and affinities: locally in Dorset - and elsewhere.

Pencil on paper, 45 x 50 cm, 2019

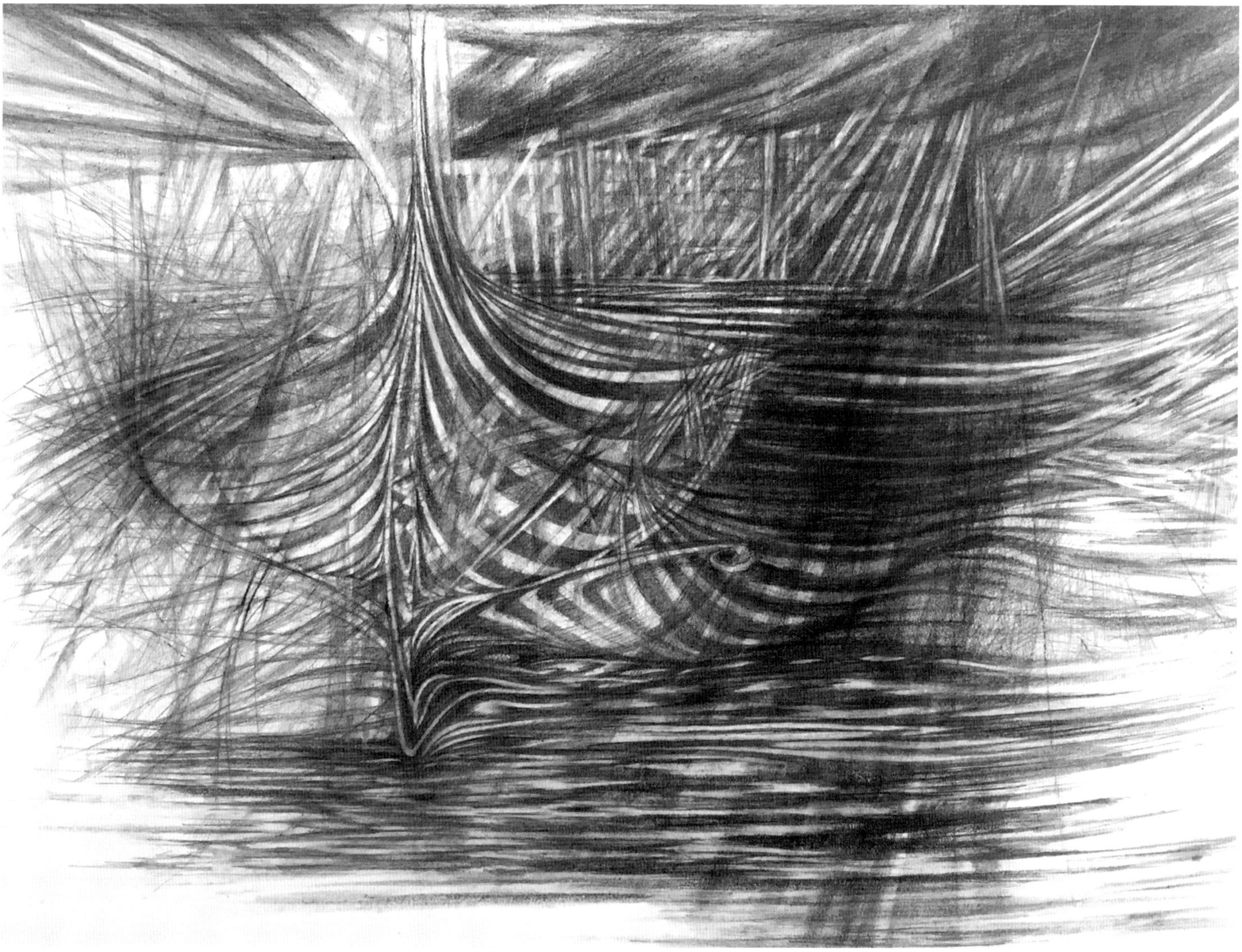

Jeremy Gardiner

The Great Globe from the West II

As an island nation, our coastline is a record of social, geological and economic change. I am exploring the modern-day reality of coastal locations; looking afresh at the harbours, bays, castles and follies that characterise our remarkable shoreline, encountering a landscape reshaped by man and touched by memories of generations past.

Watercolour with jesmonite and acrylic on handmade cotton rag paper, 30 x 42 cm, 2018

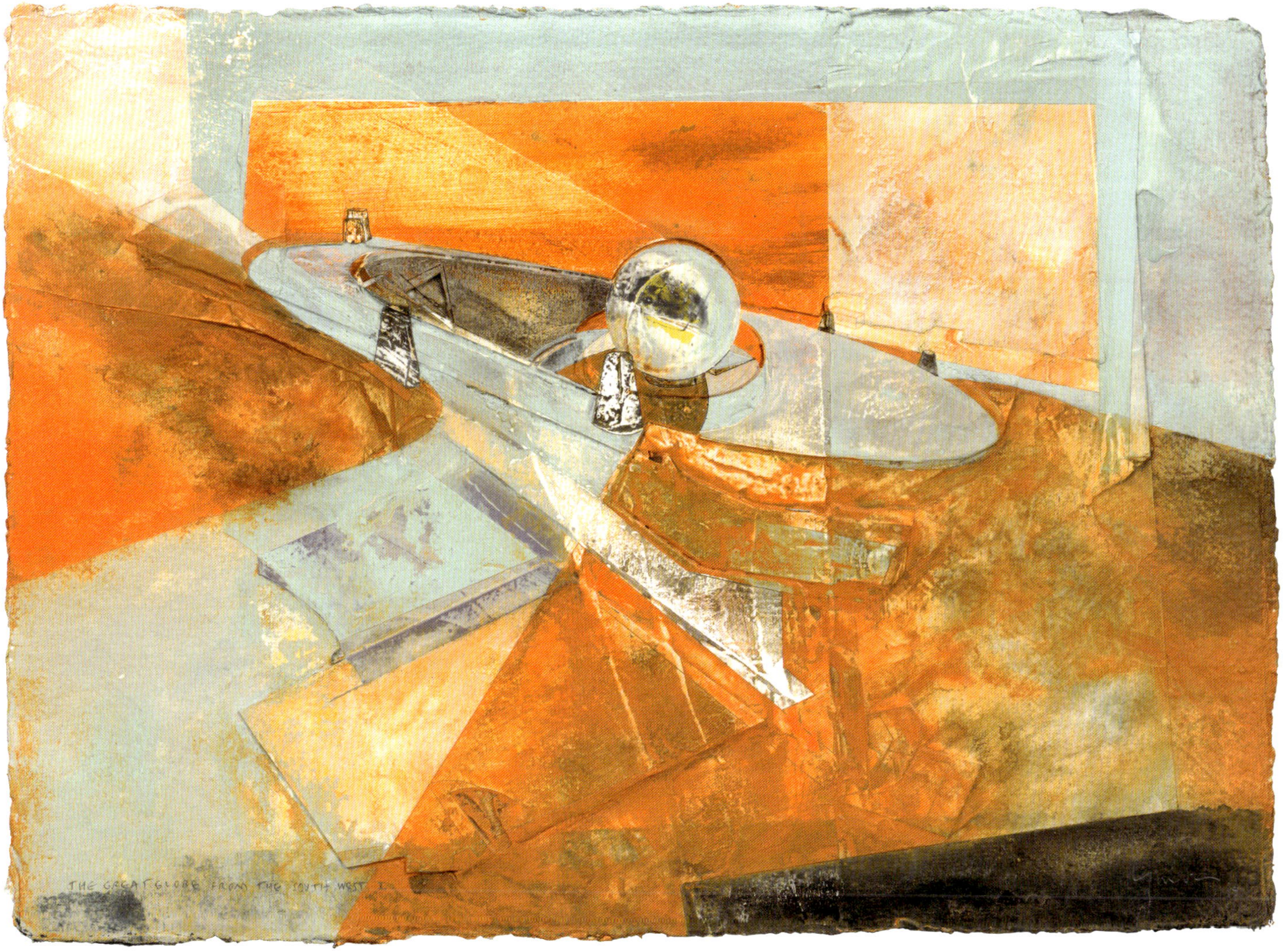
THE GREAT GLOBE FROM THE SOUTH WEST I

Jindra Jehu
Ocean Drifter, Portland Bill

Ocean drifters stranded by the tide
Littoral litter
Seaweed bound
Journeys told in tangles and twists of rope net and line

Collected isolated scrutinised
Unexpected grace observed

Choreography of oceanic forces
Dancers shaped by timeless rhythms
Tide current and race

Ink, charcoal and chalk on watercolour paper, 152 x 121.5 cm, 2016

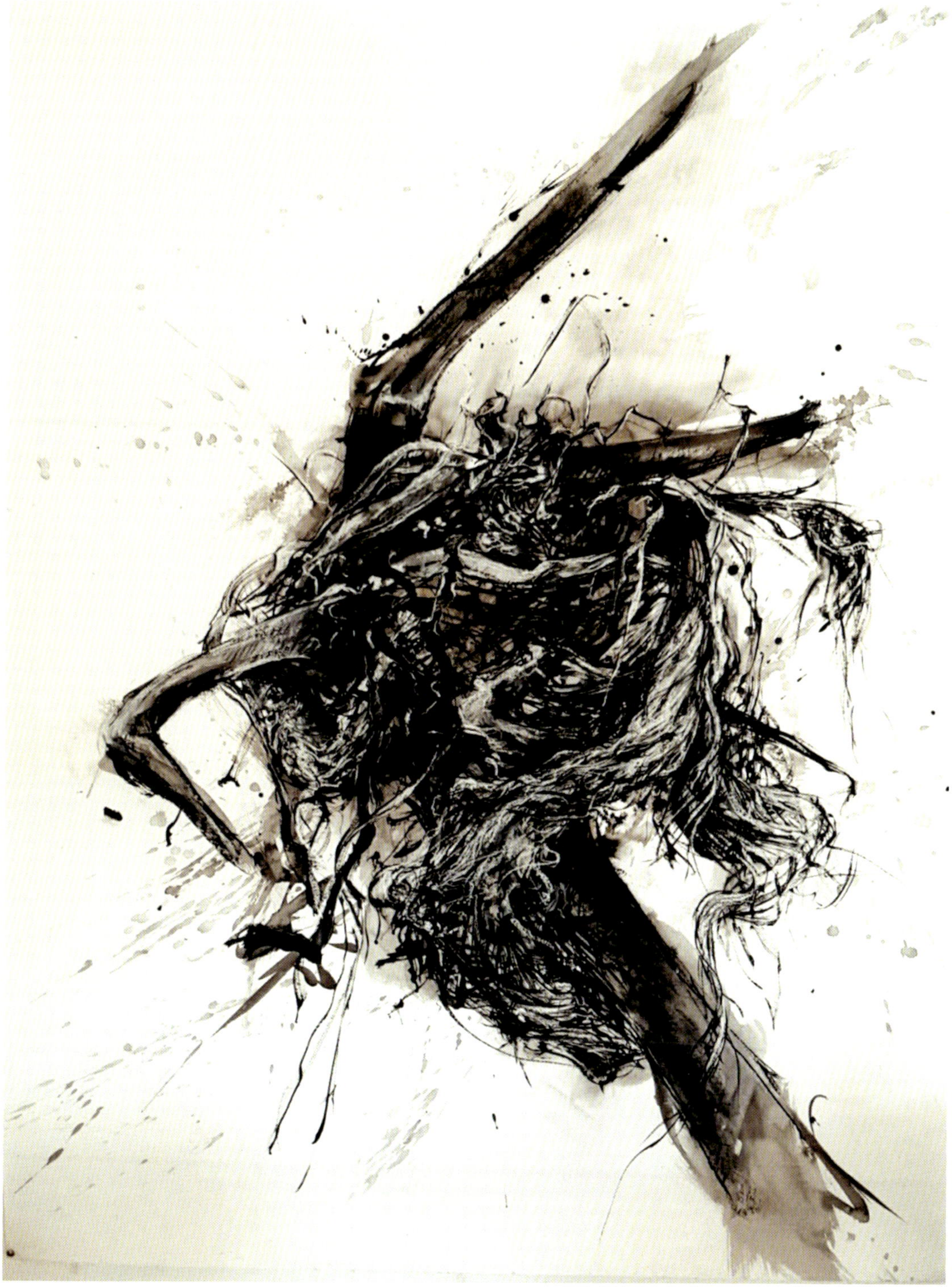

Julia Hutton

Burning Light, Siesta

The drawing is from a continuing body of work entitled *Burning Light*.

The hand drawn burnt line has been critical in the articulation of my thoughts and intentions, to capture the essence of sunlight and express ideas related to our changing world, time, place and memory. Research into Met Office sunshine data has also influenced the development of my work.

Burnt line drawing on paper, 30 x 30 cm, 2017
(Shortlisted for Jerwood Drawing Prize)

Katy Shepherd

Mother Drawn From My Memory

The drawing belongs to an ongoing project to create images from fading recollections of my mother, over twenty years on from her death in 1996. I have used only my memory banks for reference and have not looked at a photograph of her for over two years.

Dry point print on paper, 41 x 31cm, 2016

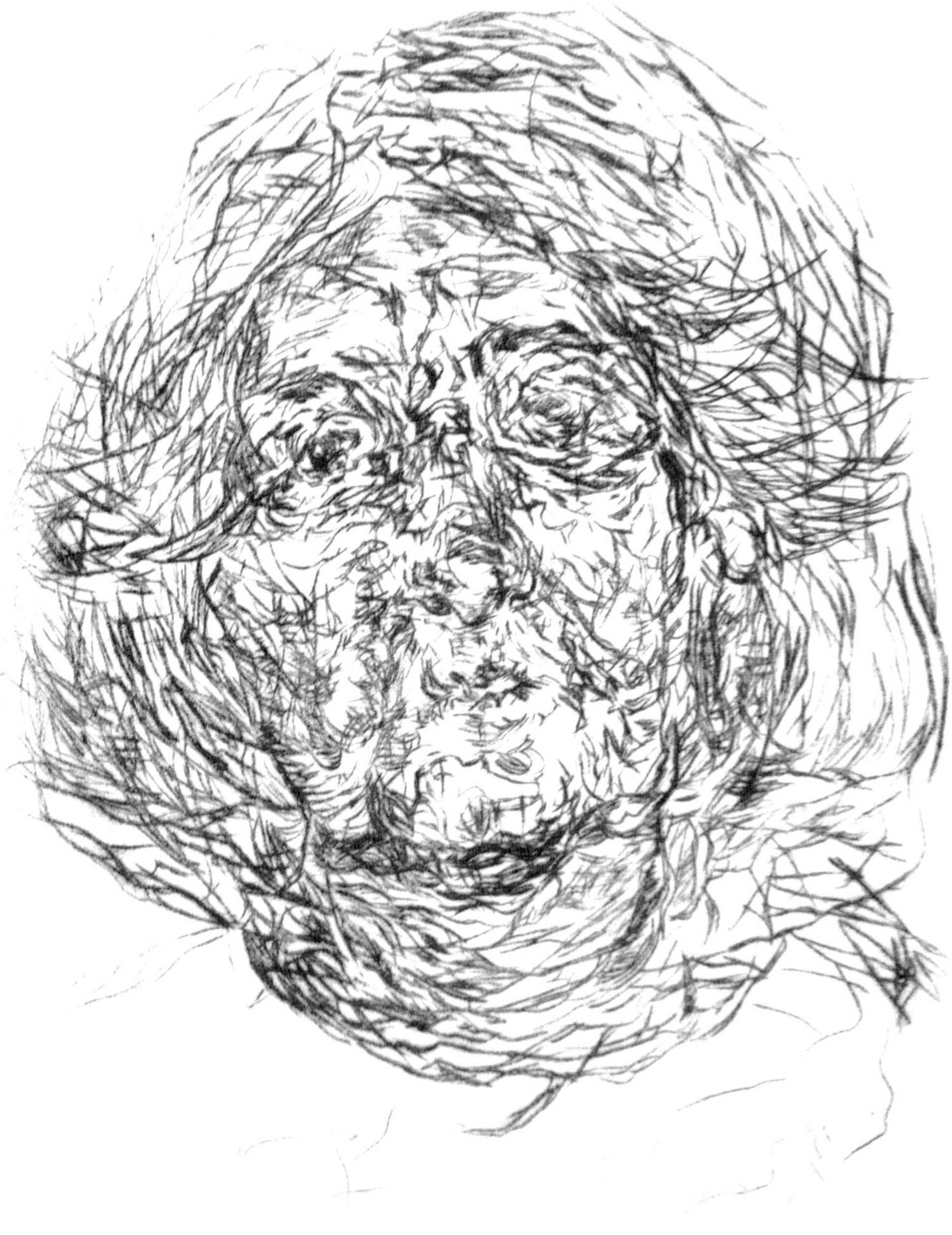

Lisa Richardson

Work 7

I think through drawing. I begin to understand my place in the world. It informs and feeds my sculptural practice, creating possibilities and fresh narratives. The Dorset landscape provides continuity, history and a site for my body to exist in.

Watercolour and pen, 25 x 17.5 cm, June 2018

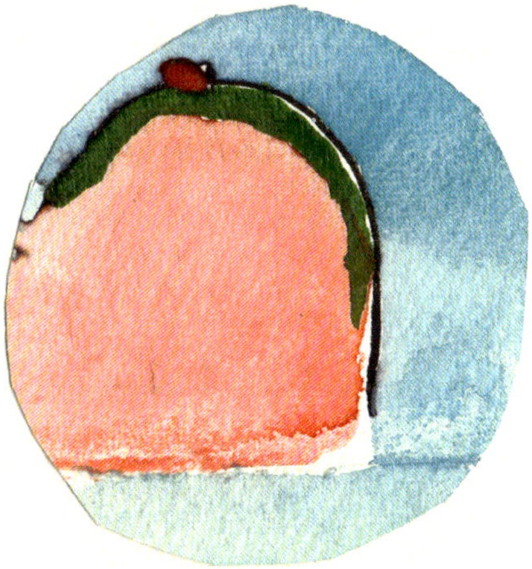

Martyn Brewster

Coastline 6, Dorset Cliffs

I have been drawing the Dorset landscape, particularly the coastline, for thirty years. Drawings vary from very large scale atmospheric charcoal works to small ink and wash studies. I make direct, intense, black and white drawings outside inspired by the endless shapes, and the ever changing shadows and light.

Ink and wash, 21 x 15 cm, 2017

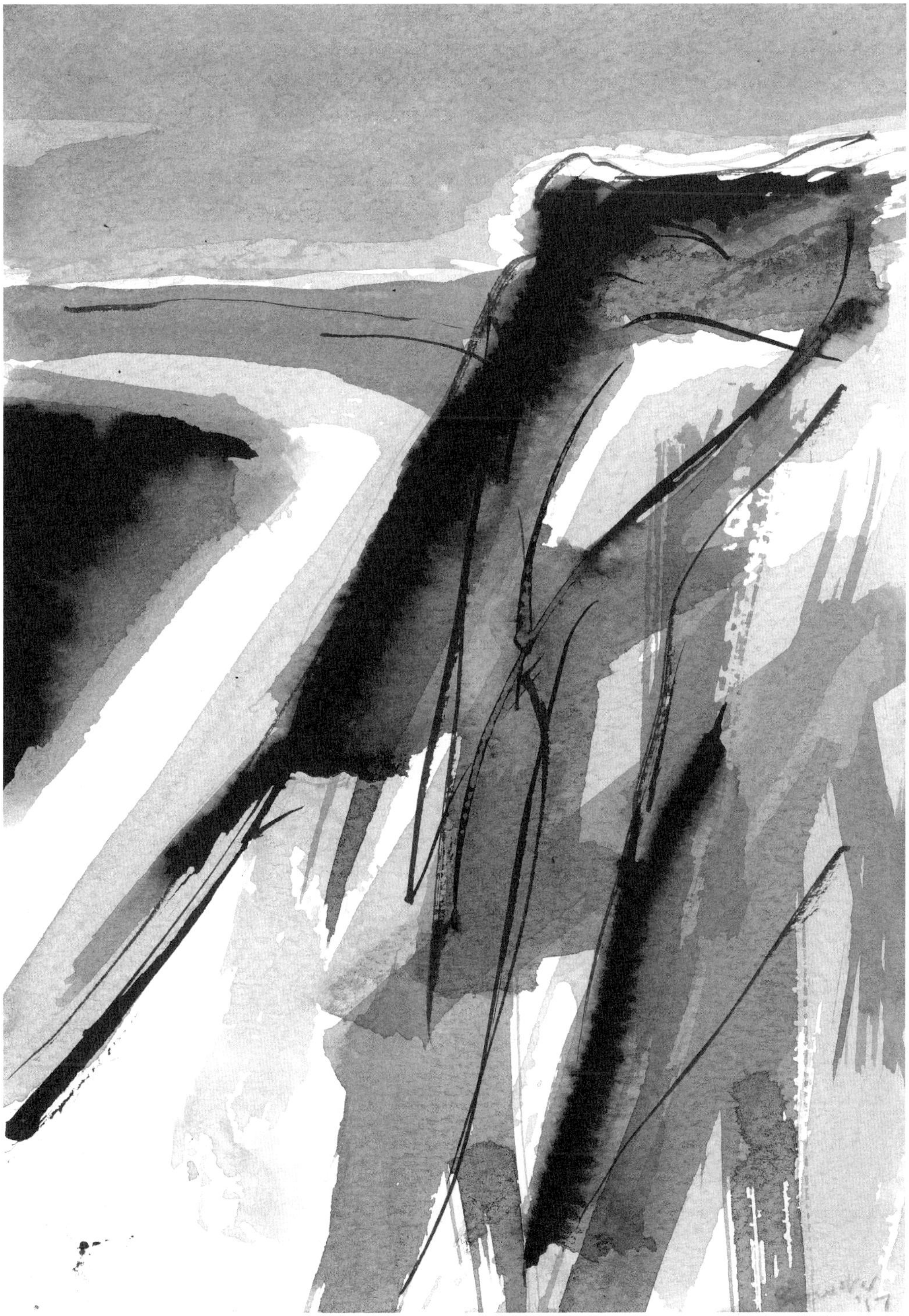

Maureen Nathan

Sherborne Nuns

I draw and paint. My work is informed by memory and the world around me. I am open in my outlook and relentless in my practice, following my own interests: intently haphazard.

Ink on paper, 25 x 25 cm, May 2018

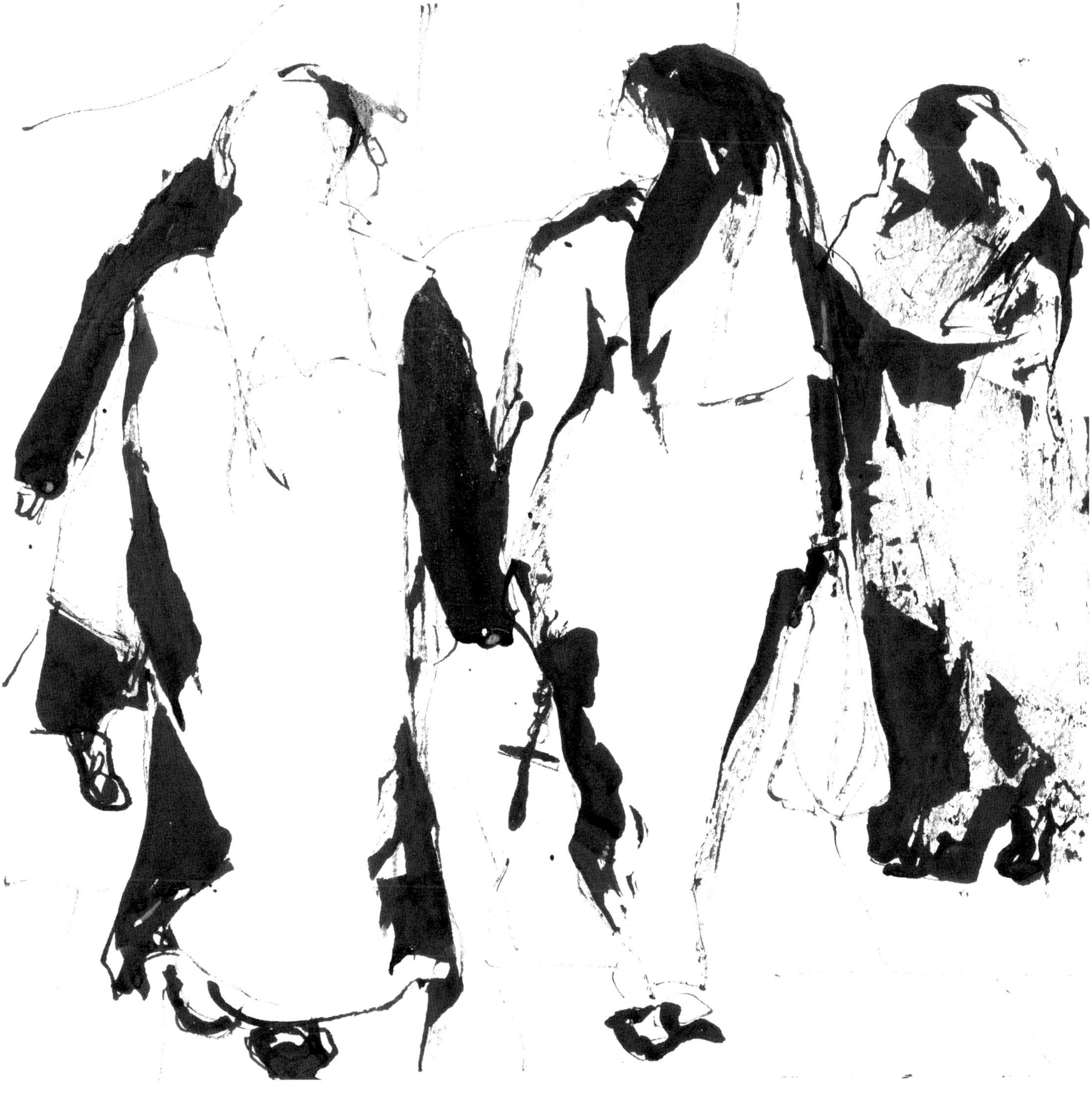

Paul Newman

Under the Oath Tree

A response to the Tolpuddle Sycamore, under which the Martyrs met. It is a story passed down through my family; from my grandfather telling me about the struggles of the Martyrs to my father taking me to see the tree. A tree as witness, document and storyteller; events entwined and embedded in its growth.

Graphite on Bristol Board, 25 x 30 cm, 2018

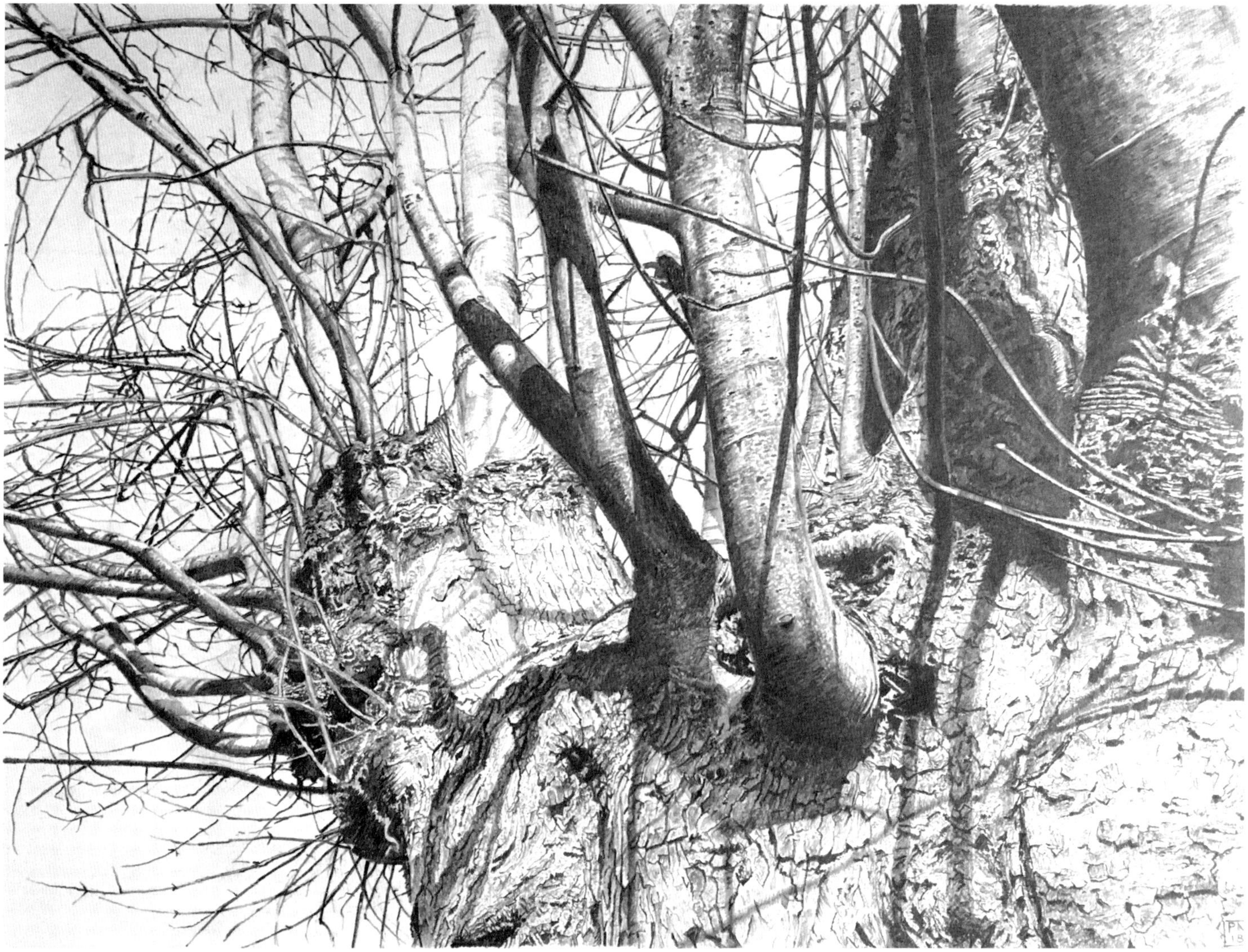

Sarah Hough

Moment 52

Once a week for a year, and whatever the weather, I made the journey to Shard Point on Brownsea Island to draw and collect sound. Walking across the island enabled my senses to become attuned to sound, wind, scent and colour, all of which find their way, directly or indirectly into my work.

Image still from the film: 'Moment 52: A Year of Drawing at Shard Point, Brownsea Island', 2019

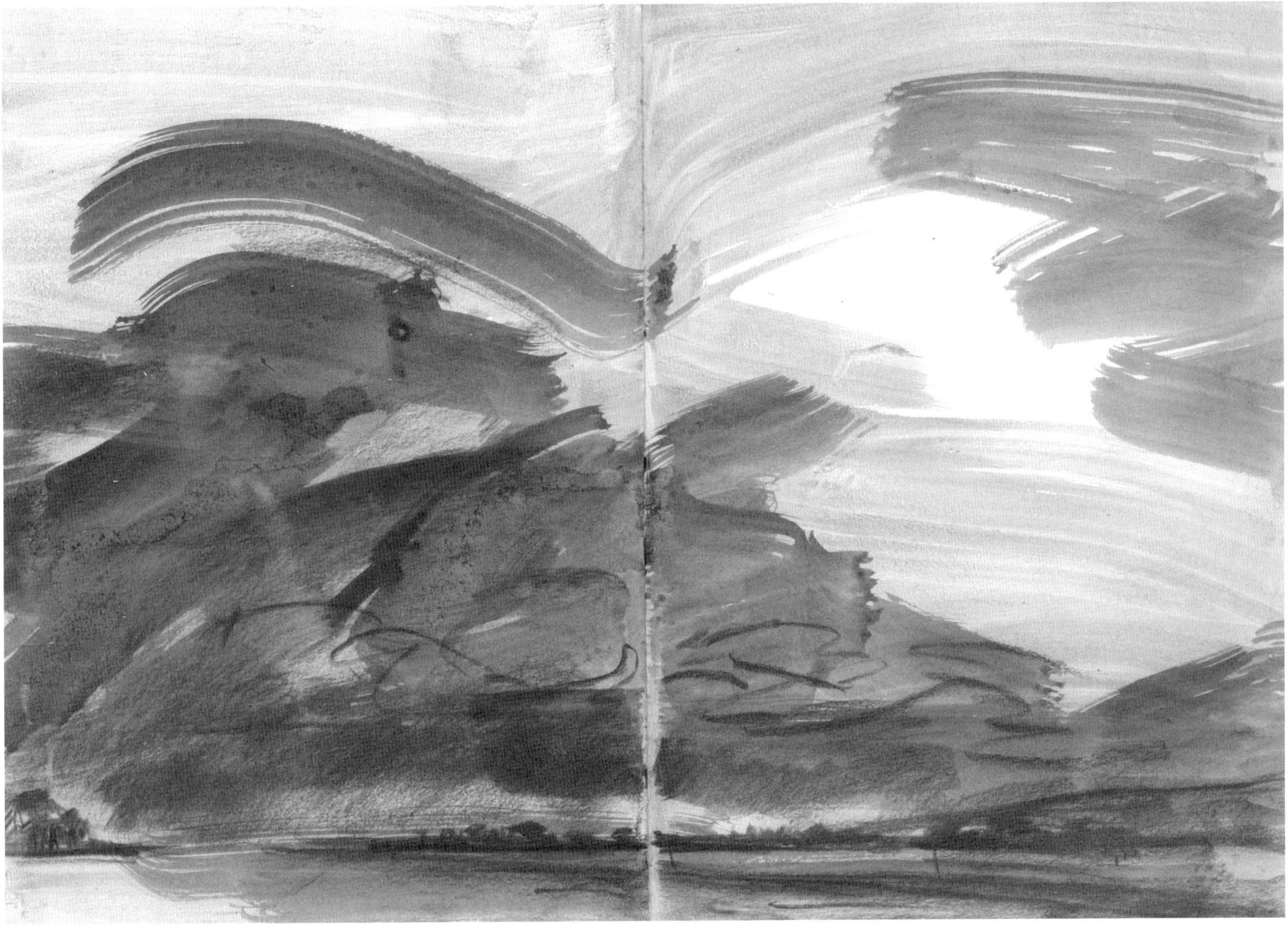

Su Fahy

Harvest

2B pencil lines en plein air where the Erica blooms. Damp heathland mimics the habitat of a palimpsest, layers of pattern, marks, plant forms, a reading of edges from the sunlight to cyanotype paper. Photogenic drawings are a homage to Fox Talbot, inspiring the photograph to become a drawing board.

2B pencil, Arches watercolour paper, cyanotype exposed en plein air, found sepia photograph, gold pen, 1940s watercolours, linen thread, in silver roundel glass frame, 22.5 x 22.5 x 12 mm, 2019

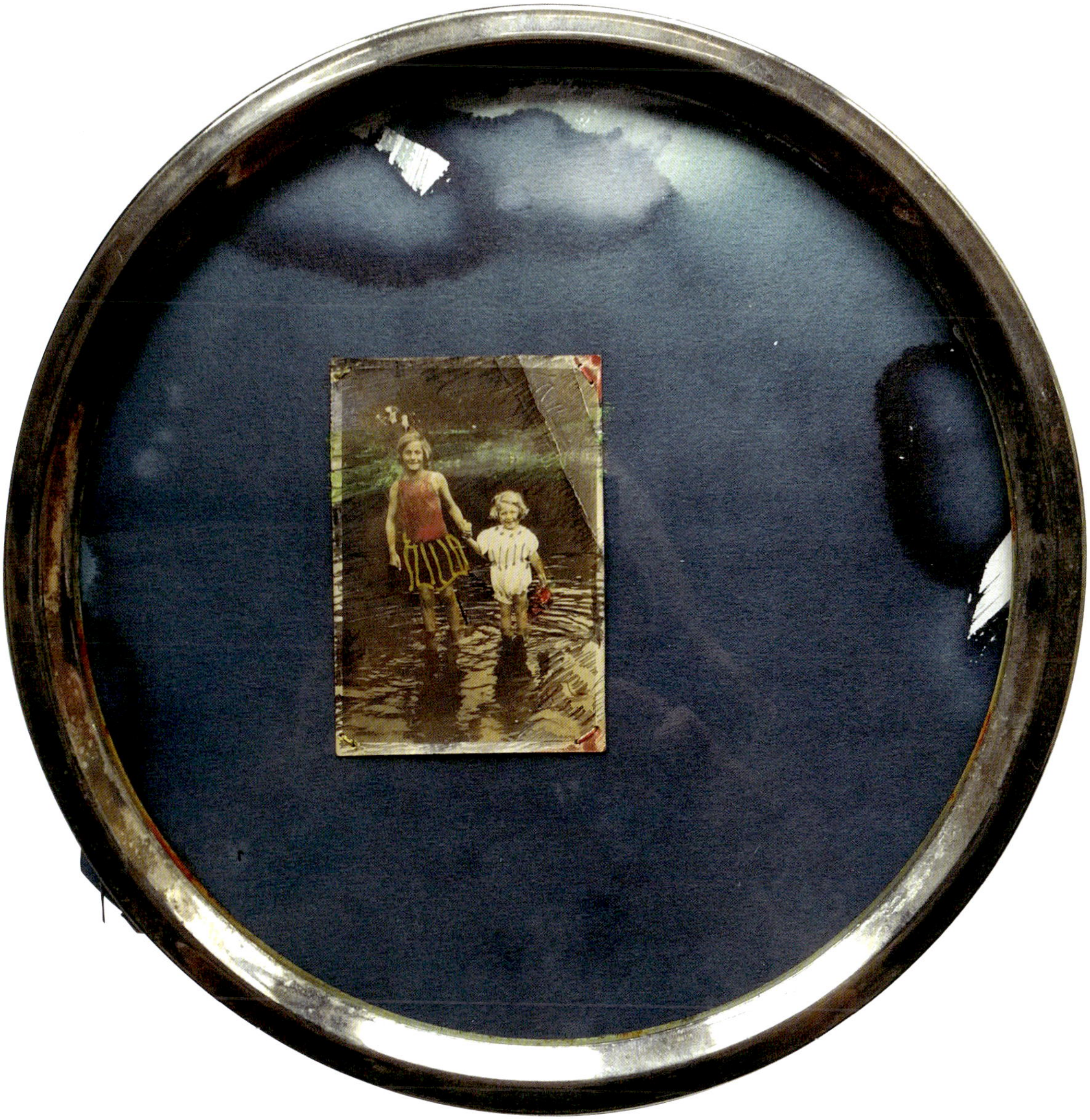

Biographies

Amanda Wallwork RWA

Amanda's practice is concerned with a continuing enquiry into landscape - her work a quest for a real understanding of what lies beyond the aesthetic. Most of her work originates from investigating the geology and archaeology of Dorset, referencing deep time and our impact on the earth.

amandawallwork.com

Andy Fung MA

Andy Fung is a psychedelic artist and musician living and working in Cardiff, Wales. He has shown extensively both nationally and internationally. Selected shows: 'Hard Edged', group show, Cardiff, 2018; Installation for Cardiff Contemporary based on Arthur Machen's book 'The Hill of Dreams', 2016; Solo show, Uni Gallery, Gothenberg, Sweden, 2013; 'May you live in interesting times' billboard commission, Cardiff, 2009; 'Plant Techtonics', Solo show at the Red Gallery, Hull, 2005; 14th International Exhibition of Wall Drawings, Reijka, Croatia, 2004.

@andyjfung

Angela Charles

A 1989 graduate of Goldsmiths College, Angela Charles moved from Brighton to the West Country in 2001. Her solo exhibition at Dorset's Sherborne House in 2003 revealed her first works inspired by the local landscape. Angela continues to exhibit successfully throughout the UK. Most recently her work was exhibited alongside Victor Pasmore's in St Ives.

angelacharles.com

Anna Morris MA

Anna Morris, MA Painting UAL, Wimbledon 2006. Lives in Somerset, draws in the Dorset landscape. Recent exhibitions: New English Art Club (NEAC) 2019, Bath Society of Artists; Bath Open Art Prize 2018 (Prizewinner); Black Swan Open, Frome 2018 (Double Prizewinner); Millfield Open, Street, 2018; Coast, Kings College Taunton (Solo) 2017; Royal West of England Academy, Open, Bristol, 2017; Wells Art Contemporary 2016.

annamorris.info

Bonnie Brown MA

Studied at Winchester School of Art. Has been a Visiting Lecturer at Winchester, Maidenhead, Chelsea Schools of Art, Southampton Institute of Art and an Associate Lecturer at the Arts University Bournemouth. Work in private and public collections in UK, EU, Canada and the USA. Lives and works in Swanage, Dorset.

bonniebrown.co.uk

Caroline Liddington MA

My early training was in Fine Art (Painting) at Byam Shaw in London during the 1980s, I then specialised in Illustration at Kingston University (BA) and Authorial Illustration at UC Falmouth (MA). Since moving to Cornwall, then Dorset in 2015, I have concentrated on oil painting and have exhibited widely.

carolineliddingtonart.com

Carrie Mason MA

Carrie Mason is a visual artist living and working in West Dorset. She graduated with a Masters in Fine Art from the Arts University Bournemouth in 2017. Her drawing practice combines repetitive and systematic mark making with an experimental approach to using materials and tools.

carrie-mason.com

Chris Dunseath FRSS, RWA

Educated in Dorset then Yeovil College, Cheltenham and The Slade Schools of Art. Exhibited widely and locally at Parnham; Sherborne House; Deans Court; Town Mill Gallery. Winner of Marshwood Vale Awards and Dorchester Arts Solo Exhibition at Duke's, Dorchester (2018). Prizewinner at The Open West and WAC. Collections: ACE and The Royal Collection.

axisweb.org/p/chrisdunseath

David Atkins

The tradition of landscape painting has always been at the heart of my drawing and painting. Living in Dorset has provided me with a rich and varied source of inspiration for my work. I work directly in the landscape, visiting many places in Dorset and experiencing them in ever changing weather and seasons.

david-atkins.com

Day Bowman B.Ed, BA

Day Bowman is a painter whose work lies on the axis of figuration and abstraction. Her current body of work questions our notion of the coast and asks is it now more border than holiday destination? Selected for b-side Festival Olympic Sailing Events 2012; Nord Art Germany 2013; tour of four museum galleries in China 2017/18; Anima Mundi Painting Prize 2019 (Winner); Venice Biennale 2019, Bath Arts Open (First Prize, Painting). Work in public collections worldwide.

daybowman.com

Debbie Lee MA

For as long as I can remember the visual language of drawing has been a way of communicating my thoughts about the world around me. I trained at the Glasgow School of Art where I developed a strong foundation in drawing. I live in Dorset balancing creativity with family life.

debbieleeart.co.uk

Ed Frith BA, FHEA

Ed Frith is an architect and teacher at the Arts University Bournemouth, where he runs the Masters in Architecture. He practices, with choreographer, Caroline Salem, as movingarchitecture.com, they are based in Clarence Mews, London. They work across art, performance and 'body building' locally and internationally.

movingarchitecture.com

Elaine Collett MA

I have lived in North Dorset since 1985, far longer than I have lived anywhere else. The Stour, the greenness, the poetry, all have influenced my work. I have a Fine Art degree from the University of Reading and MA in Fine Art from Arts University Bournemouth.

dorsetshire.com/emc

Emma Davies BA, FRSA

Born in Leeds, Emma moved to Dorset when nine years old. After studying at Bournemouth and Poole College of Art and Design she moved to the Midlands, gaining a degree in Visual Arts in 1993. Within a few years, Emma plans to move back to her spiritual home, the Purbecks.

emma-davies.com

Fay Stevens BA, MA, PGCTLL

I am an archaeologist, artist, curator and writer. My work is about senses of place: a process of excavation unravelling layers of time, memory and substance. I have researched and mapped the Bronze Age landscapes of Dorset and currently walk the Jurassic Coast as an embodied cartography of space.

cargocollective.com/FayStevens

Faye Bowden BA

Faye Bowden is a Dorset based artist who graduated from Arts University Bournemouth in 2015. Her practice is largely process based, mostly involving repetition - sometimes as content but more often as creative strategy. Drawing, in its broadest sense, is integral to Faye's practice and is often where her inspiration comes from.

fayebowdenart.com

Fiona Campbell MFA, MRSS

Currently based in Somerset, Fiona takes inspiration from her natural surroundings, often collecting found objects from her locality, and on walks along the Dorset coast. Alongside her own art practice, she works within the community running workshops. She has an MFA and won a RSS Gilbert Bayes Award, 2019.

fionacampbellart.co.uk

Fiona Robinson MA, RWA

Exhibitions: 2019 Pushing Paper, British Museum; 2018 Centro Internazionale d'Arte di Palazzo Te, Mantua, Italy (Solo); Women with Vision, RWA Bristol. 2016 Derwent Drawing Prize; The Drawing Museum Laholm Sweden. 2012 Jerwood Drawing Prize. Awards: Drawing Prize RWA Bristol 2011; Prizewinner 4th International Drawing Biennale Sydney, Australia 2007; University of Bath Painting Prize First Prize, 2007. Major Collections: British Museum, London, Fitzwilliam Museum Cambridge, Swindon Museum and Art Gallery, Polish Art Foundation Melbourne Australia, RWA Bristol.

fionarobinson.com

Fran Norton

Dr Fran Norton is an artist, writer and lecturer specialising in drawing. She uses printing, photography, writing, installation, film, stitch, burning, touch-screens and other embodied processes, to draw. In collecting, documenting and re-presenting everyday archives, her practice attempts to articulate the socio-political spaces, concepts and interrelations shaping contemporary living experiences.

frannorton.net

Fran Quinlan BA

I moved to Dorset from London in 1987 to live by the sea. Whilst walking, I take in the smells and the sounds of the sea, wind and landscape, which fill me with a sense of connection to nature and inspire me to dwell upon matters of the human condition.

Frances Hatch MA

Frances was born in Cambridgeshire. Her studio is in Weymouth. She studied at Aberystwyth UCW, Goldsmiths' College and Wimbledon College of Art (MA in Printmaking). Contributor: Drawing and Painting: Materials and Techniques for Contemporary Artists (T&H). Award: The Shenzhen International Watercolour Biennial Prize 2016 (Royal Institute of Painters in Watercolours).

franceshatch.co.uk

Helen Dean BA, PGCE

Alongside maintaining my own practice I have lived and taught art in secondary schools in Dorset for the past twenty six years. Originally trained in printed textiles, for the past ten years I have mainly focused on drawing. I have exhibited in a number of exhibitions locally and further afield.

helendeanart.co.uk

Helen Simpson

Living on a hill buffeted by weather I am very aware of an ever changing landscape. When I look closely at plants they too reflect the mysterious energy and transformative power of nature. Training: Banbury College; Royal Academy Schools. Recent major solo exhibitions: Oxford Botanic Garden; Wolfson College Oxford.

helensimpsonartist.co.uk

Holly Yates

Holly Yates is based on, and inspired by, Portland. She explores the extremes of what textiles can be, by innovative and experimental work, combining fibre with other media. Drawing is at the core of all her work. Holly also works in digital textile print design and fine art printmaking.

holly-yates.com

Ilona Skladzien MA

Ilona Skladzien was born in Poland and moved to Dorset in 2013 to live and work, making it her second home. She did her MA in Fine Arts at Arts University Bournemouth. Her current mixed media works and drawings are informed by psychology and mass media imagery, specifically YouTube.

ilonaskladzien.com

Jem Main MA

Art education: Birmingham, Portsmouth, Liverpool; later gaining an MA in Museums and Galleries in Education. Taught and lectured, but achieved an 'unusual' career in art education, encompassing all phases of formal education and in other spheres. This culminated in the realisation of The Study Gallery, Poole and appointment as Founding Director.

creative-helix.com

Jeremy Gardiner

The artwork of Jeremy Gardiner is held in corporate and public collections, including BNP Paribas, the Government Art Collection and the V&A. Recent exhibitions include 'Tintagel to Lulworth Cove' at The Nine British Art, St James's, London. In 2020 a monograph will be published by Sansoms to coincide with a touring exhibition of his work.

jeremygardiner.co.uk

Jindra Jehu BA, PGATC

Jindra Jehu studied art in Bournemouth, Leicester and Cardiff, then taught in Hampshire. Since returning home to West Dorset in 2001 her work has been concerned with the interconnectedness of landscape and man. She combines her practice with part-time teaching and regularly exhibits in Dorset and further afield.

jindrajehu.co.uk

Julia Hutton MARCA

MA Royal College of Art, London (2001-3). Selected exhibitions: Trinity Buoy Wharf Drawing Prize (2018); Jerwood Drawing Prize (2017, 2016 , 2015); The Observatory Prize, Exeter University (2017); Drawing Biennial, RWA (2017, 2015); Royal Academy Summer Exhibition (2017, 2014, 2013, 2012, 2011); Discerning Eye, London (2017); The Threadneedle Prize, London (2012). Work is held in the collections of Royal College of Art and British Museum Drawing Collections.

juliahutton.co.uk / thedrawingworks.com

Katy Shepherd MA

Katy grew up in Christchurch, moving to London in her twenties where she gained an MA in painting at the Royal College of Art. During the 1990s she expanded her practice to include animation and has exhibited successfully in London for over twenty years before returning to Dorset to live.

katyshepherd.co.uk

Lisa Richardson MA

Lisa Richardson's Fine Art practice encompasses Drawing, Sculpture and Photography. Richardson explores the potent relationship between the landscape, the maternal body and the act of creativity. Her work is often simultaneously absurd, humorous and poignant. She studied at The Cheltenham School of Art and The Slade School of Art, and is Course Leader for MA Illustration at the Arts University Bournemouth.

lisarichardson.me

Martyn Brewster MA, ATC

I moved to Dorset in 1988, and taught part-time at the Arts University Bournemouth until 2004. A professional painter all my life with work in public collections, including V&A, British Museum, Pallant House and Hepworth Wakefield. Also major retrospectives at Russell Cotes Art Gallery and Museum (1977) and RWA (2001) and featured in Vivienne Light's book 'Re- Inventing the Landscape, Contemporary Painters in Dorset' (2001).

martynbrewster.org / waterhousedodd.com

Maureen Nathan

Life events delayed my formal entry into the art world until the 1990s. Spending time in Dorset as a young adult down from London had a huge impact on me. Settling here eventually the landscape and walks have played a great part in my development as an artist.

maureennathan.com

Paul Newman

I am intrigued by our relationship with nature, through understanding a particular place over time or sometimes through chance encounters. Trees are unique products of their environment. I grew up in Dorset so the Tolpuddle Sycamore was never far away; the idea of what it might represent has always remained with me.

paulnewmanartist.com

Sarah Hough

The drawing is always about the 'moment', what is happening right here right now, and how that makes me feel. It's those raw, powerful and elemental moments that remind me what a privilege it is to be alive - a tiny part of the cyclical force of nature.

sarahhough.com

Su Fahy DPhil, MA, ARPS, SFHEA

Su Fahy is an artist working in lens-based media, principally photography, drawing, and sculpture. Fahy's research utilises the aura of the documentary photographic image in order to interrogate and contextualise our readings of natural environments. Working principally to commission, Fahy engages with sense of place, and archive materials.

@memoryartpalace

Dorset Visual Arts

Dorset Visual Arts is a charitable membership organisation with an educational remit. This is largely expressed through activities and events that bring artists to the attention of the public in ways that promote a better understanding of their work. Establishing a Dorset connection in what we do is important both in terms of revealing the range and profile of artists living and working here, but also in building creative relationships with artists working elsewhere.

This publication is the second in an on-going series of books that explore an art form or creative movement. The first, *Fifty Dorset Makers* profiled the work and individual businesses of designer makers.

This is differently conceived and sets the tone for future publications. Here, the work was submitted following an open call and selected by four, independent artists working in academic and curatorial roles. The selection aims to survey the wide variety of concepts and forms drawing takes and is contemporarily explored. The publication has been funded by the selected artists. A stock of books is allocated to each artist, the residual share of the edition being sold on behalf of DVA to further its charitable aims.

DVA is open to all artists. It manages various project groupings, some open access, some by selection to a relevant criteria. DVA also produces Dorset Art Weeks, the renowned, biennial Open Studio Event.

Jem Main

Creative Director, Dorset Visual Arts

www.dorsetvisualrts.org

Drawing on Dorset

Selected by

Anita Taylor
Executive Dean of Bath School of Art and Design and founding Director of the Trinity Buoy Wharf Drawing Prize

Tania Kovats
Artist and Professor of Drawing at Bath Spa University

Deborah Harty
Artist and Researcher

Tim Knowles
Artist and Curator

Advisers to the project

Simón Granell MA

Dr. Fran Norton

DORSET VISUAL ARTS

EVOLVER

ARTS UNIVERSITY BOURNEMOUTH

PH MEDIA

FINE FAMILY FOUNDATION

S&G STEPHENS & GEORGE